OXFORD THEOLOGICAL MONOGRAPHS

Editorial Committee

Oxford Theological Monographs

RITUALISM AND POLITICS IN VICTORIAN BRITAIN

The Attempt to Legislate for Belief

BY

JAMES BENTLEY

1478
1978

OXFORD UNIVERSITY PRESS

Oxford University Press, Walton Street, Oxford OX2 6DP

OXFORD   LONDON   GLASGOW   NEW YORK

TORONTO   MELBOURNE   WELLINGTON   CAPE TOWN

IBADAN   NAIROBI   DAR ES SALAAM   LUSAKA

KUALA LUMPUR   SINGAPORE   JAKARTA   HONG KONG   TOKYO

DELHI   BOMBAY   CALCUTTA   MADRAS   KARACHI

© *Oxford University Press 1978*

British Library Cataloguing in Publication Data
Bentley, James
    Ritualism and politics in Victorian
    Britain.—(Oxford theological monographs.)
    1. Ritualism—Political aspects 2.
    Church of England
    I. Title   II. Series
    264'.03   BX5123   77–30353

ISBN 0 19 826714 2

*Printed in Great Britain by
Billing & Sons Limited, Guildford, London and Worcester*

TO MY WIFE,
WITH IMMENSE GRATITUDE

PREFACE

IT has been said that the Conservative ministry of 1874 to 1880 'got off to a quiet start'.[1] This was not the impression of those who lived through it. Thirty years later Archbishop Randall Davidson remembered the religious and political events of 1874 as the stormiest he had known.[2] In that year the Government had decided to crush ritualism in the Church of England by passing the Public Worship Regulation Act, as a result of which no fewer than five Anglican clergymen were sent to prison.

Because 1874 was the last time religion occupied the entire attention of a British parliament, the events surrounding the Public Worship Regulation Act offer an opportunity unique in recent history for studying the interaction of politics, theology, and popular religion. This book first tries to explore how this interaction reached the point where Parliament felt impelled to pass such an act. Next it examines the behaviour, in public and behind the scenes, of those who brought the act into being and those who opposed it. Thirdly it shows how the ritualist clergy destroyed the act by determined civil disobedience, so that ritualism continued to exercise the minds and passions of leading politicians and churchmen until well after the death of Queen Victoria. Lastly it pursues the religious and political consequences of the whole controversy, which were not only quite different from those intended by the promoters of the 1874 Act, but also of unexpected value to the Church.

Some of the unpublished material in this field was mined by Professor P. T. Marsh for his biography of Archbishop Tait,[3] and I can add nothing to what he found in the Disraeli papers. The papers of Archbishop Tait, however, have provided much information that would have been outside the scope of Professor Marsh's study. In addition I have been able to use the papers of the first Lord Cairns, which have only recently been

---

[1] H. Ausubel, *John Bright, Victorian Reformer*, 1966, p. 189.
[2] Report of the Royal Commission on Ecclesiastical Discipline, 1906, 12923 (m).
[3] P. T. Marsh, *The Victorian Church in Decline*, 1969.

made available at the Public Record Office. These reveal, for instance, how Disraeli's government was prepared to mislead the Archbishop of Canterbury in order to get its own way in matters that seriously affected the Church. The papers of the fourth Marquess of Bath proved surprisingly revealing, being perhaps unduly neglected because of the remoteness of Wiltshire! As well as giving information about the religious situation in an important area, they pin-point a crucial moment in the political career of the third Marquess of Salisbury which has never hitherto been connected with the quarrels over the Public Worship Regulation Act. Lord Salisbury's own papers have provided abundant material, and I have derived important information from the Gladstone Papers in the British Library. As these papers show, Mr. Gladstone's attempt to find a *modus vivendi* between warring parties in the Church and Parliament was at times extremely harrowing for him.

To avoid the lop-sidedness which comes from quoting only the partisan religious newspapers of the time or else *The Times* (as if it somehow represented the country as a whole), I have used as much as possible the columns of the provincial press. Finally, my research has been particularly enriched by the nineteenth-century material in the John Rylands Library, Manchester, and by the collection of theological pamphlets at Pusey House, Oxford.

JAMES BENTLEY
The Vicarage
1977   *Oldham Lancashire*

ACKNOWLEDGEMENTS

I SHOULD like to thank the staff of the libraries and archives I consulted, as well as the National Trust for permission to see the Beaconsfield papers at Hughenden Manor. Without generous permission to work in the Bodleian, the British Library, Lambeth Palace Library, Pusey House, the Public Record Office, and the John Rylands University Library at Manchester, I could not have completed my research for this book.

I thank Mrs. Mary Colville for permission to quote from the papers of her great-grandfather, Archbishop Tait, and Sir William Gladstone, Bart., for permission to quote from the Gladstone manuscripts in the British Library. I am indebted to the Marquess of Salisbury for permission to consult and quote from the Salisbury papers now at Hatfield House, and to the Marquess of Bath for permission to consult and quote from the Bath papers at Longleat House. At the time of my research the Salisbury papers were at Christ Church, Oxford; the librarian and staff went to great trouble to make it easy for me to work there. I am grateful for permission to quote from the Cairns papers presented to the Public Record Office in 1966 by Rear-Admiral Earl Cairns.

Amongst many that have helped and encouraged me, I should like to thank particularly five persons: the Revd. Dr. T. M. Parker, Professor J. Simmons, the Revd. W. R. L. Watson, Mr. Desmond Heath, and Mr. Stephen Medcalf. I express my gratitude for the secretarial help of Mrs. Janice Stott. I record, too, my thanks to the staff of Oxford University Press, whose care has greatly improved my book.

CONTENTS

LIST OF ILLUSTRATIONS

I

INTRODUCTION

The Mid-Victorian Church

'YOUR railroad starts the new era,' wrote W. M. Thackeray.[1] Certainly, as the railways transformed the English countryside they helped to transform the English Church as well. They sped everywhere, and with them sped the bishops and clergy. Samuel Wilberforce, Bishop of Oxford from 1845 and of Winchester from 1869, was the first churchman to exploit them to the full, visiting every corner of his diocese and bringing together his clergy in conference and retreat, and in the course of a railway journey lasting a couple of hours he would dash off two or three dozen short letters.[2] Other bishops followed his example. Improved episcopal activity was generally thought to be a good thing by the parochial clergy. But what if one disapproved of one's bishop, or suffered his disapproval?

Scope for disapproval and disagreement was immense. The period of excitement caused by the intellectual and spiritual renewal in Oxford in the 1820s and 1830s had not come to an end. The religious revival brought about by the Oxford Tractarians provoked immense hostility. According to Thomas Arnold, 'the fanaticism of the English High Churchmen' had become 'the fanaticism of mere foolery. A dress, a ritual, a name, a ceremony, a technical phraseology,—the superstition of a priesthood without its power—. . . would make no man the wiser, or the better.' Arnold called Keble, Pusey, Newman, and their fellow Tractarians, 'The Oxford Malignants'. His biographer, A. P. Stanley, Dean of Westminster, found his

---

[1] W. M. Thackeray, 'De Juventute' (1860), in *Roundabout Papers, Works* xii, 1898, p. 232.
[2] J. W. Burgon, *Lives of Twelve Good Men*, 1888, ii. 36.

views on this subject to be a trifle strong;[1] but Stanley, and other Broad Churchmen like him, none the less had themselves little time for the exclusive attitudes of the High Church party.

The Evangelical party of the Church of England expressed its hostility quite as fiercely as Arnold had done. Though still dominant in the Church, Evangelicalism was proving in some respects unstable. In an Evangelical household the two authorities were the Bible and the father. By the middle of the nineteenth century the authority and indeed the truth of the Bible were no longer certain, and it has been suggested that if the Oedipus complex is ineradicable, the Evangelical system perhaps involved a serious error in its insistence on the absolute authority of the father.[2] In 1851 Charles Kingsley noted that 'the young men and women of our day are fast parting from their parents and each other; the more thoughtful are wandering either towards Rome, towards sheer materialism, or towards an unchristian and unphilosophic spiritualism.'[3] Evangelicals deeply felt the loss of such people. They felt betrayed by High Churchmen whom they supposed to be leading the young to Rome. Their suspicions were confirmed when men like Newman and Manning became Roman Catholics. In any case their belief in individual conversion and the experience of salvation implied that no priest could possibly come between a man and his God. Trollope's Mr. Slope in *Barchester Towers* accurately portrayed Evangelicalism in its attitude to the High Church followers of Dr. Pusey:

With Wesleyan Methodists he has something in common, but his soul trembles in agony at the iniquities of the Puseyites. His aversion is carried to things outward as well as inward. His gall rises at a new Church with a high pitched roof; a full-breasted black silk waistcoat is with him a symbol of Satan; and a profane jest-book would not, in his view, more foully desecrate the Church seat of a Christian, than a book of prayer printed with red letters, and ornamented with a cross on the back.

[1] A. P. Stanley, *The Life and Correspondence of Thomas Arnold, D.D.*, 2nd edn., 1890, p. 257, where the passage in the text is quoted from Arnold's article 'The Oxford Malignants', *Edinburgh Review*, Apr. 1836.

[2] A. O. J. Cockshut, *Truth to Life: The Art of Biography in the Nineteenth Century*, 1974, p. 66.

[3] In the preface to his novel *Yeast*.

Yet the High Church movement continued to appeal to many. It brought Romanticism to the service of religion (an element derived largely by John Keble from Wordsworth and Coleridge).[1] No other party in the Church tried to live by what Newman described as 'the sacramental system; that is the doctrine that material phenomena are both the types and instruments of real things unseen';[2] yet this principle was immensely attractive to many contemporary Christians. Mr. Gladstone, for example, visiting Naples in 1832, had been overwhelmed by a vision of Christianity as a 'ministry of symbols, its channels of grace, its unending line of teachers from the Head: a sublime construction based on historical fact.'[3] Only Tractarianism shared this kind of vision.

In consequence, those outward symbols—dress, ritual, ceremonies—which Thomas Arnold described as mere foolery were crucial channels of grace to the Tractarians. As the movement developed, every motion or gesture of the priest at the altar, every item of his dress as he celebrated Holy Communion, became meaningful. Dr. Pusey initially deprecated seeking to restore to the Church the richer style of vestments used in the reign of Edward VI: 'our own plain dresses', he wrote, 'are more in keeping with the state of our Church, which is one of humiliation.'[4] His views did not prevail.

The tendency towards more gorgeous vestments and more elaborate ritual gained impetus from the Tractarians' study of church history. This aspect of their thought was part of their attractiveness to many Victorians. They were attempting to find a 'better' basis for the insights of Evangelicalism, looking to history for the pure and authentic Church. Not only Tractarians did this. George Eliot in Coventry constructed a historical chart of the first six centuries A.D. which finally showed that there had never been a pure and authentic Church at all. Dean Stanley had possessed a similar chart at Christ Church.[5] The conclusions of the Tractarians were not so despondent.

[1] See G. K. Clark, 'The Romantic Element, 1830–1850', in *Studies in Social History*, ed. J. H. Plumb, 1955, pp. 211–39.
[2] J. H. Newman, *Apologia Pro Vita Sua*, 1864, ch. 1.
[3] J. Morley, *The Life of W. E. Gladstone*, 1903, i. 87–8.
[4] H. P. Liddon, *Life of E. B. Pusey*, 1893, ii. 142.
[5] H. House, 'The Quality of George Eliot's Unbelief', in *Ideas and Beliefs of the Victorians*, 1949, pp. 159–60.

William Stubbs's inaugural lecture as Regius professor of
modern history at Oxford in 1866 declared that 'The study of
modern history is, next to theology itself, the most thoroughly
religious training the mind can receive.'[1] (At Oxford, of course,
modern history meant chiefly medieval history.) Thirty years
earlier Pusey, Keble, and Newman had started the 'Library
of the Fathers'—a series which consisted in all of forty-eight
volumes and ended in 1885. According to Newman's *Apologia*,
a study of the ante-Nicene Church of Alexandria was what
confirmed his own ideas of the sacramental principle.

All this coincided with a parallel reform of the Church of
England. Under the initial impetus of Sir Robert Peel in the
1830s and 1840s a tremendous effort was made to extend the
Church. Between 1840 and 1876 well over 7,000 churches
were restored and another 7,000 built at a cost of more than
£25,500,000.[2] The ritualist and ceremonial revival coincided
with the Victorian era of prosperity, which lasted from 1851 to
1873. Money was available to build churches more in keeping
with the new ideas. All Saints', Margaret Street, for example,
built in 1859, was paid for mostly by the banker Henry Tritton;
but a considerable sum was also provided by the Conservative
Member of Parliament A. J. Beresford Hope (who took charge
of the accounts). The baptistry was paid for by the Marquess of
Sligo, and the stained glass in the south aisle was largely
provided at the expense of the daughters of the Earl of Wicklow
and by the incumbent (the Revd. W. Upton Richards).[3] The
period provides countless examples of similar generosity.

By 1876, eight theological colleges had been founded, and
the number of Anglican clergymen was rapidly increasing.
About 3,000 new benefices had been created. In addition, the
abolition of pluralities released about 4,000 more. In 1841 (the
date of the first accurate official returns) there were 14,613
Anglican clergymen; by 1871 the number had risen to 20,694.

The ubiquitous railways brought these men together. The
Convocations began to meet again for the first time for over

---

[1] Quoted in G. P. Gooch, *History and Historians in the Nineteenth Century*, 2nd
edn., 1952, p. 341.

[2] G. K. Clark, *The Making of Victorian England*, 1962, pp. 152–8 and 169 f.
N. Gash, *Sir Robert Peel: The Life of Sir Robert Peel after 1830*, 1972, especially pp. 99 ff.

[3] The *Builder*, 4 June 1859, p. 377.

130 years. Diocesan conferences and church congresses began to meet regularly. And meetings heightened party feelings. Soon groups of clergymen and their lay supporters formed associations with the sole object of attacking their theological rivals. At the same time, a society flourished outside the Church precisely to attack the Establishment. (It had been formed after the Anglicans of Leicester, in an attempt to preserve their own political supremacy, had gaoled a Congregationalist draper. His minister, E. T. Miall, formed the Anti-State Church Society, which in 1853 became the Liberation Society.)

There were now not enough bishops to control ...se Anglican clergy. At the Church Congress of 1861 the Hon. C. Lindsay asked for 130 more! All that happened was the creation of the suffragan sees of Dover and Nottingham in 1870, to be followed by Guildford in 1874, Bedford in 1879, and Colchester in 1882. The new diocese of Truro was created in 1877, followed by four others in the 1880s. This was still barely enough; but it soon became clear that the revived and reformed episcopate *wanted* more control over the inferior clergy.

Mostly they (and many others) wanted to control High Churchmen. The High Church movement had already weathered a number of powerful attacks. Pusey himself had been condemned by the Vice-Chancellor of Oxford and six doctors of divinity for preaching in 1843 a sermon on 'The Holy Eucharist, a Comfort to the Penitent'; he had been suspended from the university pulpit for two years.[1] Now the increase in ritual was alarming the general public again. Lady Charlotte Guest in her diary for 15 February 1850 described the sensation caused by the Revd. Mr. Ponsonby's Ash Wednesday service in the mortuary chapel at Canford. Ponsonby placed a print of the crucifixion and two high candlesticks on the altar. 'All his demeanour too,' wrote Lady Charlotte, 'and his turning to this altar and from the people when in prayer startled them very much. It has grieved me, I cannot say how deeply. The more so, as I fear I can do nothing to rescue our people from the contamination of witnessing practices which must tend to break down the feeling against the

---

[1] Liddon, op. cit., vol. ii, pp. 306–69.

Papacy, at least in its ceremonials.'[1] For over forty years such anxieties increasingly preoccupied the Church of England.

Personalities

Anxieties about ritualism obsessed politicians as well as clergymen (for no Victorian politician dared ignore religion), and the two leading politicians of the 1870s, Gladstone and Disraeli, took opposite sides in the controversy. Gladstone had become a High Anglican at Naples in 1832 whilst reading the occasional offices of the Prayer Book. Whereas (like all Evangelicals) he had formerly taken his religion from the Bible, 'now', he wrote, 'the figure of the Church arose before me as a teacher, too.' The Church of England, he realized, was Catholic as well as Protestant, and this conviction remained with him the rest of his life. Newman's secession to Rome did not distress him: 'God who made him', he told Mrs. Gladstone, 'can make for us, if need be, others like him.'[2] (And indeed to a large extent Dr. Pusey took Newman's place.) Deeply devout, Gladstone introduced household prayers twice daily and sometimes preached at them. On Sundays he went to church twice and taught in Sunday-school. As he dressed and undressed he read from a large Bible kept on his dressing table. A few days before his seventy-ninth birthday he could argue at dinner in favour of tolerating sociable drunkenness, and then retire to a small study to read a theological book in German by his old Roman Catholic friend Dr. Ignaz von Döllinger.[3]

However much men disagreed with Gladstone, few doubted his religious sincerity; nearly everyone doubted Disraeli's. Born of agnostic parents with a Jewish background, educated by Unitarians, he had been confirmed because one of his father's friends considered it prudent.[4] Long after his death, when one might have thought that political passions had cooled, Gladstone declared that Disraeli possessed no principles or convictions of any kind, save on the subject of the Jews.[5] A Conservative bishop could write of 'the sublime unprinciple of

[1] Quoted in G. Avery, *Victorian People*, 1970, pp. 155–6.
[2] P. Magnus, *Gladstone, a Biography*, 1954, pp. 12 and 74.
[3] Ibid., pp. 50 f., 128, and 379 f.
[4] R. Blake, *Disraeli*, 1966, p. 11.
[5] Magnus, op. cit., p. 381.

Dizzy'.[1] Yet he worshipped regularly at Hughenden and took the Sacrament at Easter. His novel *Tancred*, though extremely satirical about the Church of England, none the less put forward the notion that this church was 'the main remedial agency in our present state'. By 1870 he had come to regret the novel's sarcasm. His excuse was that the Church would have been able to build up a society based on loyalty and reverence had it been properly led. Chief amongst those who had failed to lead was Newman. His secession, according to Disraeli, was a mistake and a misfortune. He and those who followed him had taken refuge 'in mediaeval superstitions, which are generally only the embodiments' of pagan ceremonies and creeds'.[2] Disraeli's Toryism involved a belief in the Church of England as 'a majestic corporation, wealthy, powerful, independent . . . one of the main guarantees of our local government, and therefore one of the prime securities of our common liberties.'[3]

By the time he took office for the last time (in 1874) he was nearly seventy. He was to die in 1881. (His wife, on whom he greatly depended, had died in 1873.) To many at this moment Gladstone seemed to be 'on the brink of Catholicism',[4] and Disraeli saw an opportunity of using the controversy over ritualism to destroy at last his political enemy.

Disraeli once told Matthew Arnold that 'Everyone likes flattery, and when you come to royalty, you should lay it on with a trowel.'[5] It needed little flattery, in fact, to enlist Queen Victoria against the ritualists. Victoria favoured the Broad Churchmen rather than the Evangelicals, observing once to Disraeli that 'The extreme Evangelical School do the Established Church as much harm as the High Church.'[6] She had taken the advice of the Dean of Windsor that 'The people of this country will undoubtedly not tolerate Ritualism, but it is equally certain that they will not put it down through the

[1] J. C. MacDonnell, *Life and Correspondence of William Connor Magee*, 1896, ii. 11. For others' doubts about Disraeli's sincerity see Blake, op. cit., pp. 48, 757, 759, and 761 f.
[2] Blake, op. cit., pp. 201 f. and 208 f., quoting from the General Preface to the 1870 edn. of Disraeli's novels.
[3] Ibid., p. 282.
[4] The *Stockport Advertiser*, 24 July 1874, p. 4.
[5] Quoted in E. Longford, *Victoria R.I.*, 1964, p. 401.
[6] Blake, op. cit., p. 511.

instrumentality of the Puritanical party.'[1] She accordingly sought other ways of putting it down. The ritualists sheltered behind the Ornaments Rubric in the Prayer Book, which allowed them to follow whatever was practised in the Church in 1549. But historians had discovered that in that year the Church of England had been far more catholic in its rituals than many now liked. One of Victoria's aims, therefore, was to alter the Ornaments Rubric, so as to 'bring the extremists back into order'.[2]

The Archbishop of Canterbury agreed with her: 'as long as the law is extremely doubtful, those who are called to administer it are in a very difficult position.'[3] Like the Queen, Archbishop Tait was Broad Church, with little time for High Churchmen. In 1841 he was one of four Oxford tutors who publicly protested against Newman's *Tract No. 90*, accusing it of 'a highly dangerous tendency, from its suggesting that certain very important errors of the Church of Rome are not condemned by the Articles of the Church of England'.[4] By the time he became Archbishop of Canterbury in 1868 he was entirely sure of himself. He recruited as his chaplain Randall Davidson, a man of similar views (if less strength of purpose[5]); Davidson became Tait's official biographer, married his daughter, and was himself later Archbishop of Canterbury.

This opposition to the ritualists was more than shared by the Evangelicals. Their leader at this time, the seventh Earl of Shaftesbury, grew up, it has been said, 'without any experience of parental love'. He was converted in the 1830s, and after this claimed to be 'an Evangelical of the Evangelicals'. In spite of his admiration for the piety and benevolence of Dr. Pusey, who was his cousin, Shaftesbury hated Tractarianism, which he described as 'the most offensive and, in many respects, the most deceitful and hypocritical' of all the '-isms' that ever existed. He never lost the delusion that the Tractarians were deliberately plotting his downfall.[6]

---

[1] *Letters of Queen Victoria*, 2nd ser., ed. G. E. Buckle, 1926, ii. 342.

[2] Ibid., ii. 300.

[3] According to the *Church Association Monthly Intelligencer*, July 1869.

[4] R. T. Davidson and W. Benham, *Life of Archibald Campbell Tait*, 1891, i. 81.

[5] This was the view of Randall Davidson's wife, who was Tait's daughter: Marie Louise, *My Memories of Six Reigns*, 1956, p. 147.

[6] G. F. A. Best, *Shaftesbury*, 1964, pp. 15, 32, and 63 f.; G. Battiscombe, *Shaftesbury, A Biography of the Seventh Earl, 1801–1885*, 1974, p. 105.

Shaftesbury also represented the conscience of Victorian England. His immense efforts in bettering the lot of the mentally sick, of children in factories, of women and children in mines, and of chimney sweeps, had made him at one and the same time imperious, arrogant, sensitive, and resentful. (Florence Nightingale said that *he* would have been put into a lunatic asylum had he not devoted himself to reforming them.[1]) He was particularly aware that some of the bishops had sadly failed to support his work: for example, once he asked Bishop Blomfield, 'Why does not my Lord of London inspect, personally, the sinks and gutters of his own miserable diocese? Alas, though he have some zeal, he has more dignity.' This experience made it hard for him to co-operate with them now in putting down ritualism. When in 1867 the House of Lords threw out his bill to alter the Ornaments Rubric, Shaftesbury attributed this to Gladstone, the Government, and the Archbishop of Canterbury. Two years later he brought in another bill to keep the ritualists in order and was conscious of similar odds: 'I shall be opposed by all the bishops, who are masters of the question, and who, secretly, abhor the measure as touching their dignity and their patronage.'[2] When the bill was lost, he vowed never again to support the Establishment.

Yet a combination against the ritualists by Shaftesbury's Evangelicals and the bishops could prove formidable. In the 1860s and 1870s the Evangelical party was showing signs of a revival. Protestant Christians had been appalled by the revelation in the religious census of 1851 that out of a population of nearly 18,000,000 only 7,261,032 persons had attended Sunday worship. They vigorously set about remedying this. In 1857, under Shaftesbury's influence, a series of special Sunday evening services took place in Exeter Hall, aimed especially at members of the working class who 'were not habitual church or chapel goers'. Over 3,000 persons attended the first of these, when the preacher was Henry Villiers, the staunchly Evangelical Bishop of Carlisle. Similar services were held in several London theatres.[3] Then in the late 1860s the Evangelicals,

---

[1] From a collection of letters sold at Sotheby's, 22 June 1976, and quoted in the *Sunday Times*, 30 May 1976, p. 4.

[2] Best, op. cit., p. 60; E. Hodder, *The Life and Work of the Seventh Earl of Shaftesbury*, Popular edn., 1893, pp. 627 and 635.

[3] L. W. Cowie, 'Exeter Hall', in *History Today*, June 1968, p. 395.

influenced by American missionaries, began to run missions at the seaside, aimed largely at children.[1] In 1873 Dwight L. Moody, accompanied by Ira D. Sankey, arrived from America to preach (and sing) biblical religion. 'The largest buildings could not hold the crowds that flocked to hear him, and at the close of every meeting hundreds of inquirers stayed for personal instruction.'[2]

Amongst those who preached at Exeter Hall were Dr. Hugh McNeile and the Revd. Hugh Stowell. McNeile dominated the religion of Liverpool from 1834 until Disraeli made him Dean of Ripon in 1868. Stowell similarly dominated Salford. When he preached at Exeter Hall, it is said that 'the May meeting audiences were entirely at his mercy; they wept or laughed, or emptied their purses just as he desired.'[3] Both men hated ritualism. Both triumphed in cities where Ulster Orangemen held sway. Macaulay unkindly said of McNeile's preaching, 'The Orangeman raises his war-whoop; Exeter Hall sets up its bray.'[4] But McNeile was important. He was the favourite preacher of Lord Cairns, the M.P. for Belfast, who married his niece and later became Disraeli's Lord Chancellor and leader of the Conservative party in the House of Lords.

Nonconformists shared both this Protestant revival and this hatred of ritualism. In 1853 the Baptist C. H. Spurgeon, for instance, began his immensely successful preaching ministry at New Park Street Chapel in London. Within two years his congregation had outgrown the chapel and moved to Exeter Hall while its own place of worship was being enlarged.[5] Spurgeon's denunciation of ritualism was both pious and violent. Speaking at Accrington in 1874, he said that when the ritualists make a wafer of bread and then worship it and then eat it, 'they have gone to a length that I think must provoke God'. In one of his most famous sermons he compared them to the nine lepers healed by Jesus, none of whom returned to give thanks to their healer: 'Nine obey ritual, where only one praises the Lord.'[6] Such views were entirely acceptable to many

---

[1] G. R. Balleine, *A History of the Evangelical Party*, 1908, p. 249.

[2] Ibid., p. 251; cf. pp. 250-4.   [3] Ibid., p. 203.

[4] Quoted in J. B. Atlay, *The Victorian Chancellors*, 1906-8, ii. 307, n. 1.

[5] Cowie, art. cit., p. 394.

[6] The *Western Gazette*, 31 July 1874, p. 6; C. H. Spurgeon, *The Treasury of The New Testament*, n. d., ii. 59.

of the country's leaders. Sir William Harcourt, Lord Ebury, Lord Sandon, and others of that stamp, as well as lesser Members of Parliament like Mr. Newdegate and Mr. Holt, had long felt that the doctrines of the Tractarians were far too close to those of Rome. As Lord Mounteagle said, they had begun to 'dread the *Tracts for the Times* as much as . . . the *Secunda Secundae* of Aquinas'.[1]

Yet in spite of this Evangelical revival, men feared that the Catholic party in the Church of England was gaining the upper hand. James Anthony Froude, who had reacted strongly against his own early Tractarianism and that of his brother Hurrell, wrote in 1873 that 'What these gentlemen have accomplished is the destruction of the Evangelical party in the Established Church.' In 1881 he declared that 'at present there is scarcely a clergyman who does not carry in one form or another the marks of the Tractarian movement'.[2]

The movement had certainly converted some notable men, including the future Conservative Prime Minister Lord Salisbury. Salisbury went up to Oxford two years after Newman's secession, where he joined the surviving Tractarians. Throughout his life he was a frequent communicant, during the week as well as on Sundays. He shared the dogmatism of the Tractarians. 'The dream of undogmatic religion', he wrote, 'is too baseless to impose long upon educated minds'—a view he retained for the whole of his life.[3] Having served in Disraeli's 1867 Cabinet, he had split from the Prime Minister over the Reform Bill, taking with him General Peel, the Secretary for War, and Lord Carnarvon, the Colonial Secretary. 'This is stabbing in the back,' Disraeli had said. 'It seems like treachery.' If Disraeli attempted to put down the ritualists, Salisbury would in all likelihood try to stab him in the back again. In doing so he could reasonably look for the support of a good number of Conservative politicians who were also High Churchmen, such as Lord Bath, Earl Nelson, the Earl of Devon, and (in the Commons) A. J. B. Beresford Hope and A. E. Gathorne-Hardy.

[1] Hansard, 3rd ser., lxxxi, 4 June 1845, p. 79.
[2] J. A. Froude, *Short Studies on Great Subjects*, new edn., 1893, iii. 172 and iv. 311.
[3] *Quarterly Review*, July 1865; cf. his views in *Quarterly Review*, Oct. 1873 and Oct. 1883, reprinted in *Lord Salisbury on Politics*, ed. Paul Smith, 1972, pp. 325, 354, and 355.

The feeling that the Tractarian movement was gaining the upper hand was further reinforced by the confident assertiveness of some of its clergy. Amongst the younger ones, the Revd. C. F. Lowder temporarily lost his licence to officiate in the diocese of London after he had given boys sixpence each to throw rotten eggs at a sandwich-man who was parading on behalf of an enemy churchwarden.[1] Older men showed their pugnacity in other ways, for instance, the Revd. G. A. Denison, Vicar of East Brent, Archdeacon of Taunton and a gradual convert from Tractarianism to ritualism, would have been deprived of his living in 1856 for attacking the Thirty-nine Articles had not the prosecution failed on a legal technicality.

A decade later a similar prosecution became a *cause célèbre*. In 1867 the Vicar of Frome Selwood in Somerset, the Revd. W. J. E. Bennett, published an open letter to Dr. Pusey called *A Plea for Toleration in the Church of England*. Bennett's letter argued that the body and blood are actually (and not only figuratively) present in the sacrament of Holy Communion. In the eyes of many this savoured far too much of Roman Catholicism, but the attempt to prosecute him for heresy before the Judicial Committee of the Privy Council failed. G. M. Young commented that in reaching its decision 'The Privy Council had rendered it so difficult for a Churchman to be a heretic that prosecutions for heresy almost ceased, and the public mind turned with the greater avidity to the persecution of ritualism.'[2] The history and consequences of that persecution form the subject of this book.

Piety and Pugnacity

By the time the Victorians took to persecuting ritualism, the ritualists were ready for it. They believed religion was serious enough to fight about. One of their leaders, a Scotsman named A. H. Mackonochie, said as much: 'The last thing an Englishman likes to do is spend his money and get nothing in return; and yet Englishmen, even City men, will spend thousands of pounds to fight about religion.'[3] Ritualist piety, like Tractarian piety before it, was schooled on John Keble's *Christian Year*.

---

[1] O. Chadwick, *The Victorian Church*, 3rd edn., 1971, i. 497.

[2] G. M. Young, *Victorian England, Portrait of an Age*, 2nd edn., 1953, p. 120.

[3] A. H. Mackonochie, *First Principles versus Erastianism*, 1876, p. 14.

Although that volume carried the epigraph, 'In quietness and in confidence shall be your strength', and aimed at exhibiting the '*soothing* tendency in the Prayer Book', it also warned Christians not to expect comfort in this life:

> Mortal! if life smile on thee, and thou find
>   All to thy mind,
> Think Who did once from Heaven to Hell descend
>   Thee to befriend;
> So shalt thou dare forego, at His dear call,
>   Thy best, thine all.

> 'Now, Christians, hold your own—the land before ye
>   'Is open—win your way, and take your rest.'
> So sounds our war-note; but our path of glory
>   By many a cloud is darkened and unblest.[1]

Far from regretting Newman, the ritualists bought and read his Anglican sermons, which were based on the pugnacious belief that 'it would be a gain to this country were it vastly more superstitious, more bigoted, more gloomy, more fierce in its religion than at present it shows itself to be'.[2] Some of them were prepared if necessary to follow Newman out of the Church of England. One wrote to Gladstone in 1875 that he did not greatly care whether three or thirty of his parishioners were empowered to prosecute him if they wished; such treatment could not destroy ritualism. 'Ritualists may be crushed and driven out from us,' he declared. 'And whither are they to go? And whose fault will it be if they follow the great man who was similarly (in effect) dealt with 20 years ago?'[3]

This devout pugnacity, which was characteristic of nearly every ritualist, can be illustrated by a closer study of three of them, the Revd. John Mason Neale, Archdeacon George Anthony Denison, and Fr. Alexander Heriot Mackonochie, whose characters were in other respects quite different. Of the three Neale was by far the most learned. As well as being a hymnologist in his own right, he translated and introduced

[1] J. Keble, *The Christian Year*, 1827; the poems quoted are for the Wednesday before Easter and the First Sunday after Trinity.

[2] J. H. Newman, *Parochial and Plain Sermons*, 1908 edn., i. 320.

[3] Gladstone Papers, British Library, Additional MS. 44444, John Oakley to Gladstone, 15 July 1874.

into the Church of England hymns and liturgies from the Latin
and Eastern Churches. He translated pious works by worthies
like the Anglo-Catholic Lancelot Andrewes, and the Roman
Catholic monk of Cluny, Bernard de Marlaix.[1] As a Cambridge
undergraduate, he helped to form and lead the Camden Society,
which was devoted amongst other things to the renewal of
church architecture. Along with Benjamin Webb he translated
The Symbolism of Churches and Church Ornaments by William
Durandus, a thirteenth-century bishop. Their aim in doing so
was to encourage the return of 'sacramentality' in church
architecture, so that every aspect of a properly designed place of
worship would speak of 'the Blessed Sacraments of the Church'.[2]
Churches designed on such principles were the ones so much
deplored by Trollope's Mr. Slope. Neale and Webb explained
that, although they were 'not prepared to say that none but
monks ought to design Churches', in their opinion patrons
should look 'at least for Church-membership' from those they
employed as architects. 'A Catholic architect', they asserted,
'must be a Catholic at heart.'[3]

Rather than mingle with none but monks, Neale found a
further vocation as spiritual director of the Sisters of St. Margaret, an order he established at East Grinstead in 1854. (Lord
John Manners had founded the first Anglican Sisterhood in
1844, as a memorial to the poet laureate, Robert Southey;
W. J. E. Butler started another group at Wantage in 1848,
and T. T. Carter a third at Clewer in 1851.) To the sisters,
Neale preached sermons allegorizing the Song of Songs. Thus,
on the third Sunday after Easter, 1857, he took the text, 'Let
Him kiss me with the kisses of His Mouth; for Thy love is better
than wine'. Applying the sacramental principle to the lips of
Christ, Neale told the sisters that a kiss from the Saviour
(involving as it did the use of *both* his lips) would remind them
of the great mystery of his two natures, one human, the other

---

[1] *Sequentiae ex missalibus . . . Recensuit, notulisque instruxit J. M. Neale,* 1852;
Carols for Christmastide, set to ancient melodies, 1853; *Mediaeval Hymns and Sequences,*
trans. J. M. Neale, 1867; *The Liturgies of SS. Mark, James, Clement, Chrysostom and
Basil, and the Church of Malabar,* trans. J. M. Neale and R. F. Littledale, n. d.;
The Private Devotions of Lancelot Andrewes, trans. J. M. Neale, new edn., 1898.
[2] W. Durandus, *The Symbolism of Churches and Church Ornaments,* trans. J. M. Neale
and B. Webb, 1843, pp. xxi and xxvii.
[3] Ibid., pp. xxi f. and xx.

divine. He urged them to 'enter into the very Holy of Holies—
when that Head which, for us, bowed down upon the cross,
shall then, in the Beatific Vision, kiss us with the kisses of His
Mouth.'[1] Hostile observers frequently accused him of abusing
his position in the Sisterhood. For example, when one of the
sisters died, her father accused Neale of first forcing her to leave
her money to the Sisterhood and then making her nurse a
patient with scarlet fever.[2]

In fact the chapels of these Sisterhoods suffered none of the
restraints of ordinary parish churches. Neale could introduce
whatever ceremonies he pleased. He was constantly at odds
with his bishop, Gilbert of Chichester,[3] but these controversies
in no way deterred him. As a High Churchman (who had tried to
work with him) wrote, Neale had ' a great theoretical admiration
of Episcopacy with a gift of insulting all embodied Bishops'.
The same critic added: 'His historical lore, which is great, is
altogether subservient to his own one-sided propagandism . . .
Politically he always takes up any cause or interest, which is
emphatically and patently un- or anti-English. Personally he is
tall and lank and hawk-faced; he snuffles and talks through his
nose, and he preferentially wears at all hours tail dress coats.'[4]

Clearly Neale could annoy, although ritualists who neither
snuffled nor talked through their noses shared his attitude to
Anglican bishops. All that the bishops know, one of them
wrote to Lord Salisbury, is 'the result of representations made
to them by their chaplains and other parasites and "expectants",
who hover about their palaces'.[5] High Churchmen had openly
distrusted bishops since the celebrated Gorham dispute, which
came to a head in 1850. Bishop Phillpotts of Exeter had refused
to institute to the living of Brampford Speke the Revd. G. C.
Gorham, believing him to be unsound on the doctrine of
baptismal regeneration. The Court of Arches agreed that Gorham was a heretic; but this judgement was overruled by the
Judicial Committee of the Privy Council, with the concurrence

---

[1] J. M. Neale, *Sermons on the Song of Songs*, 1867, pp. 8 and 16.
[2] Chadwick, *The Victorian Church*, i. 507.
[3] See A. G. Louth, *The Influence of John Mason Neale*, 1962, Chapter 12, 'Trouble
with the Bishop'; cf. the more detailed examination of Neale's controversies in
A. G. Louth, *John Mason Neale: Priest Extraordinary*, 1975.
[4] Louth, *The Influence of John Mason Neale*, p. 159, quoting A. J. Beresford Hope.
[5] Salisbury Papers, M/74/06/04: the Revd. J. M. Rodwell.

of the Archbishops of Canterbury and York as assessors, only
Bishop Blomfield standing out against the Privy Council. Here
were the archbishops apparently agreeing that the Church
was subordinate to the State. 'Instead of protesting they had
acquiesced in a state-controlled Christianity and a state-
tailored doctrine.'[1] Bishop Phillpotts accused the Archbishop
of Canterbury of condoning heresy, and went so far as to
declare him excommunicate. None the less Gorham was instituted.

Archdeacon Denison's reaction was typical of High Churchmen. Why, he asked, should the bishops continue to sit in the
House of Lords? People had forgotten that the Apostolic
succession of the ministry and the primacy of the sacraments
were 'the *essence* of a Church; all other things are only the
accidents of a Church', including the political appointment of
bishops. By approving of heresy in the Gorham case, the bishops
had (with one exception) virtually abdicated their office.[2]
Denison's outlook was the same a quarter of a century later:
'the "Establishment" of England, representing for the time
the Church of England, has been overcome by the World of
England, and lies prostrate at its feet.'[3]

In fact such a stance appealed to his controversial, not to
say cantankerous, nature. 'I have always set my face', he once
wrote, 'as a flint against the mind of the time.'[4] Denison was
ordained in 1832 at the beginnings of the Catholic revival in
the Church of England and (by his own admission) an 'extreme
High Churchman'.[5] 'Being of a despotic turn of mind', he
later recorded, he ruled his first church 'with an iron hand'.
He took only gradually to ritualism. Preferred to East Brent in
1845, he found what he described as 'the germ of "Ritual" in
preaching in the surplice'—a small thing inherited from his
predecessor, but 'quite enough then to convulse the country'.
Slowly his pattern of worship became more ornate. 'It takes
some digging to get at the foundations of "Ritual" ', he wrote;

[1] A. O. J. Cockshut, *Anglican Attitudes: A Study of Victorian Religious Controversies*,
1959, p. 60. Chapter 3 is devoted to the Gorham case.
[2] G. A. Denison, *Why Should the Bishops continue to sit in the House of Lords?*,
2nd edn., 1851, pp. 5, 17–18, and 27 ff.
[3] G. A. Denison, *Notes of My Life, 1805–1878*, 2nd edn., 1878, p. 349.
[4] L. E. Denison, *Fifty Years at East Brent*, 1902, p. 202.
[5] Denison, *Notes of My Life*, p. 67.

and in 1866, when a committee of Convocation reported on ritualism, he confessed, 'I had only just begun to dig'.[1]

By now, however, although his antecedents did not dispose him to what he called a 'high ceremonial', it dawned on him that 'a costly and magnificent ceremonial', as well as having precedents in Judaism and the Apocalypse, 'was the natural accompaniment and exponent of the teaching of the Doctrine of THE REAL PRESENCE'. His adoption of ritualism remained 'partial', as he said, compared with the practices followed by some of his contemporaries;[2] but this did not imply the slightest lack of commitment to their cause. He was, he announced in 1877, a ritualist 'in principle, wholly; in practice, as I have seen my way to revive and to restore'.[3]

By contrast, A. H. Mackonochie's ritualism was uncompromising almost from the start of his career. At Oxford in the mid-1840s he had come under the influence of Pusey's chief lieutenant, Charles Marriott. One of his curacies was served with Butler at Wantage (along with H. P. Liddon), another in the slums of London with the Revd. Charles Lowder.[4] Then in 1861 he became Vicar of St. Alban's, Holborn, a church built entirely according to ritualist principles.

Literally built into St. Alban's was hatred of the Gorham judgement. In August 1862 Mackonochie, dressed in surplice and stole, placed a ladder against the wall behind the font, and climbing up he inserted into a cavity a long scroll containing signatures from a huge meeting held twelve years before to condemn the judgement. Over the cavity was put an inscription: 'I acknowledge one Baptism for the remission of sins.'[5]

Mackonochie summed up his attitude to the relations between Church and State in a series of sermons preached in 1876. Whatever the State might claim in secular affairs, 'in things spiritual, as Sacraments, Worship, Faith, and the like, which belong to God only, the Church must be absolutely free'. Church discipline, he argued, bound men and women only with

[1] Denison, *Notes of My Life*, pp. 75, 95, and 347.

[2] Ibid., pp. 342 and 349.

[3] G. A. Denison, *A Charge of the Archdeacon of Taunton at his Visitation, April 1877*, 1877, p. 15.

[4] M. Reynolds, *Martyr of Ritualism*, 1965, pp. 16 and 28 f.

[5] Ibid., p. 88.

respect to the soul. The Church possessed 'no coercive jurisdiction, no power to enforce by external pressure, her judgments.
She may refuse to give Communion or other spiritual ministrations, but She cannot visit with temporal consequences
spiritual offences.'[1] No Act of Parliament could replace or
substitute for the commission of Christ. As for the bishops,
appointed by the State whether the Church wanted them or not,
'the fault in the manner of their election may be such as to
forfeit much, if not all of the spiritual graces (apart, i.e. from
sacramental gifts) which the Church can expect to receive from
them.'[2]

These views were undoubtedly coloured by the fact that for
nine years Mackonochie had himself been threatened by both
Church and State with temporal punishment for his spiritual
activities, for the Church Association had set up Mr. John
Martin, a solicitor and a nominal ratepayer in the parish of
St. Alban's, to prosecute him in the courts. The charges were
that at Holy Communion he elevated the Sacrament, knelt
excessively during the prayer of consecration, used incense,
mixed water with the wine, and put candles on the altar. The
Court of Arches condemned only the incense, adding that the
water ought to be mixed with the wine before the service began;
but the Judicial Committee of the Privy Council set this aside
and condemned Mackonochie on all counts.[3] Legally and
illegally, Mackonochie managed to avoid the consequences of
this judgement until 1882, when Archbishop Tait was dying.
Tait persuaded Mackonochie to resign by exchanging the
living of St. Alban's for that of St. Peter, London Docks. His
resignation, said the archbishop, would 'set men's minds free
for the pressing duties which devolve upon the Church in the
face of prevailing sin and unbelief'.[4]

Mackonochie came to believe that he should never have
agreed with the dying archbishop. His prosecutors continued
to hound him, and managed to secure his deprivation from
St. Peter's; he resigned to avoid any further consequences.
Many of his admirers attributed his subsequent mental wander-

[1] Mackonochie, op. cit., pp. 9 and 47.
[2] Ibid., pp. 52 and 30.
[3] Reynolds, op. cit., pp. 129, 134, and 142.
[4] Marsh, *The Victorian Church in Decline*, p. 284.

ings to the enormity of his treatment.[1] In 1887 he lost his way in a Scottish snowstorm, and froze to death.

By this time his fame was such that the poet and tragedian William McGonagall wrote an elegy on his death:

> Friends of humanity, of high and low degree,
> I pray ye all come listen to me;
> And truly I will relate to ye,
> The tragic fate of the Rev. Alexander Heriot Mackonochie.
>
> Who was on a visit to the Bishop of Argyle
> For the good of his health, for a short while;
> Because for the last three years his memory had been affected,
> Which prevented him from getting his thoughts collected . . .[2]

Canon Gregory of St. Paul's summed up his character admirably: 'a man of great force of character, of iron will and indomitable determination in all that he conceived to be his duty to his Church and his Master.'[3] This was the stamp of nearly all the ritualists who were to come under attack.

[1] Reynolds, op. cit., p. 264; P. Schaefer, *The Catholic Regeneration of the Church of England*, English trans. 1935, p. 137.

[2] 'The Tragic Death of the Rev. A. H. Mackonochie', in *Poetic Gems, selected from the Works of William McGonagall*, 1934, p. 185.

[3] *Alexander Heriot Mackonochie, a Memoir, by E. A. T.*, ed. E. F. Russell, 1890, p. 326.

II

RITUALISM

The Ritualists

NOT until the 1860s did most observers notice the change that was taking place in the High Church party. According to the *Edinburgh Review* in 1867, the phenomenon called 'ritualism' was 'of sudden growth—the work almost of the last three years'—and had 'taken the nation and Church by surprise'.[1] The great Tractarian movement, said Bishop Fraser of Manchester in 1874, had developed of late 'some strange and extravagant forms'; and in the same year Gladstone informed the House of Commons that ritualism then was quite different from the ritualism he had known twenty years before.[2]

The change was visible in the appearance of some of the younger clergy. In place of the old-fashioned clerical dress of the Tractarians, these men had taken to wearing 'jam pot' collars, long straight coats reaching down to their heels, and what the Evangelicals called 'Mark of the Beast' waistcoats (which carried up to the cravat without dividing). Such clothing, imitating the dress of Roman Catholic priests, offended many Englishmen, even though Gladstone pointed out to them that some Presbyterian and Dissenting ministers were also wearing the new kind of waistcoat.[3] Gladstone could not hide the truth that the Anglican ritualists had adopted the garb as a deliberate anti-Protestant singularity. The habit began at Cuddesdon, the High Church theological college founded in 1853; in 1858 Bishop Wilberforce told its students that their self-conscious neckcloths, coats, and whiskers were sure to annoy, and he urged them not to 'walk with a peculiar step, carry their heads at a peculiar angle, and read in a pecu-

---

[1] *Edinburgh Review*, Apr. 1867, p. 441.
[2] *Eccles and Patricroft Journal*, 10 Oct. 1874, p. 3. Hansard, vol. 220, 1874, 1376.
[3] Details of dress in Reynolds, *Martyr of Ritualism*, pp. 68 f. W. E. Gladstone in the *Contemporary Review*, 1874, p. 672.

liar tone'.[1] His advice was ignored. The semi-monastic life of Cuddesdon protected the students as yet from the criticism of the outside world, and their peculiarities were encouraged by the example of the Vice-Principal, H. P. Liddon, who, it was said, resembled at this time an Italian ecclesiastic, glittering-eyed, with 'a white band for a collar and a black cassock with a broad belt'.[2]

The outward appearance and behaviour of the ritualist clergy were matched in novelty by what they did in church. Initially, however, they failed to agree amongst themselves about this. In 1861 Mackonochie was advocating altar candles, 'some veils', ceremonial ablutions, and facing east at the Holy Communion as essential; he added that the medieval (and contemporary Roman Catholic) eucharistic vestments were also desirable.[3] In 1866 a committee which Convocation set up to consider ritual dealt with vestments, altar lights, incense, the use of wafer bread at Holy Communion, non-communicating attendance, and the elevation of the bread and wine during the service. In the same year the Revd. G. R. Prynne's *Eucharistic Manual* was advocating vestments, two lights on the altar, and incense, adding that it was usual 'to place a cross upon or above the middle of the altar'. Differences of this kind persisted until 1875, when the annual meeting of the English Church Union agreed that the ritualist clergy should adopt six main points: vestments, the eastward position, altar lights, the mixture of water and wine in the chalice at Holy Communion, wafer bread, and incense.[4] These became the main points of contention between the ritualists and their opponents.

Altar lights and vestments had been introduced piecemeal into the Church of England since the 1850s.[5] Ignorance led some of the clergy to adopt distinctly exotic vestments. R. S. Hawker, the Vicar of Morwenstow, held that the Eastern

[1] Quoted by O. Chadwick, *The Founding of Cuddesdon*, 1954, pp. 92 f., from A. R. Ashwell and R. G. Wilberforce, *Life of the Rt. Rev. Samuel Wilberforce*, 1888, ii. 367 f.

[2] F. Burnard, *Records and Reminiscences*, 1917, p. 109.

[3] Reynolds, *Martyr of Ritualism*, p. 78.

[4] G. R. Prynne, *The Eucharistic Manual*, 2nd edn., 1866, p. 15. 'Six Points' in *The Oxford Dictionary of the Christian Church*, ed. F. L. Cross and E. A. Livingstone, 2nd edn., 1974, p. 1281.

[5] Details in H. M. Brown, *The Church in Cornwall*, Truro, 1964, p. 101; S. L. Ollard, G. Crosse, and M. F. Bond, *Dictionary of English Church History*, new edn., 1948, p. 630. S. L. Ollard, *The Oxford Movement*, 1915, p. 178, n. 5.

THE · HOLY · EUCHARIST ·

Fig. 1

Four of the Six Points, illustrated in 1865.

Church was the mother of Celtic Christianity; believing it to be the custom of the east, he wore a cope, alb, and scarlet gloves for matins as well as at the eucharist.[1] Most other ritualists took to wearing chasubles.

The innovators were for the most part young men. At John Keble's funeral in April 1866, R. W. Church, the Tractarian Dean of St. Paul's, noticed alongside people whom he had always regarded as followers of Keble 'a crowd of younger men, who no doubt have as much right in him as we have, in their way—Mackonochie, Lowder, and that sort.' They were 'Excellent good fellows', he wrote; but he was conscious that they looked upon the older Tractarians as 'rather *dark* people, who don't grow beards, and do other proper things'.[2] Hostile observers regretted the fact that young men were becoming ritualists. Queen Victoria said she was 'shocked and grieved' to see 'the higher classes and so many of the young clergy tainted with this leaning towards Rome!'[3] But the ritualists themselves were proud of the fact that their movement was leaving cautious men behind and taking hold of 'strong-minded and strong-bodied' young churchmen.[4]

Victoria was right about the high social rank of the ritualists, many of whom were rich enough to remain unpaid curates all their lives. One of them was younger brother to the Queen's private secretary.[5] Nearly all were graduates of Oxford or Cambridge. In time of trouble they could deploy influential family connections. Archdeacon Denison, for instance, the ritualist Vicar of East Brent, was the son of an M.P.; his brothers included a Speaker of the House of Commons, a Bishop of Salisbury, and a Governor-General of Australia.[6] A number of ritualists were aristocrats. The Evangelical Archbishop Thomson of York had the misfortune to encounter two such men as successive deans of his cathedral—the Hon. Augustus Duncombe, who was the sixth son of Baron Faversham

[1] Brown, op. cit., p. 101. Hawker's general and increasing quaintness, not only in the matter of dress, is brought out by P. Brendon, *Hawker of Morwenstow*, 1975.

[2] M. C. Church, *Life and Letters of Dean Church*, 1895, p. 173.

[3] *Letters of Queen Victoria*, ii. 302.

[4] R. J. Wilson, *An Earnest Protest*, Oxford, 1874, p. 13.

[5] See A. Ponsonby, *Henry Ponsonby*, 1942, pp. 310 f.

[6] R. Wilson, 'Ossington and the Denisons' in *History Today*, Mar. 1968, pp. 164–72.

and married to a daughter of the Marquess of Queensberry, and Arthur Percival Purey-Cust, who was grandson of the first Lord Brownlow and married to a sister of the Earl of Darnley.[1]

This social background partly accounts for the customary self-assurance of the ritualists (and of their Tractarian predecessors). J. A. Froude said that although his brother Hurrell preached episcopacy, 'he belonged himself to the class whose business was to order rather than obey. If his own bishop had interfered with him, his theory of episcopal authority would have been found inapplicable to that particular instance.' A professed opponent of the ritualists asserted that their attitudes were 'founded apparently on the principle of universal licence and absolute lawlessness'.[2]

The ritualists appeared happy to follow this principle because they saw themselves as representatives of the supernatural, universal, and eternal Catholic Church. Since no human authority could override this Church, whoever opposed their activities was bound to be wrong. Shortly after arriving at East Grinstead as spiritual head of his Anglican Sisterhood, Neale wrote, 'I should never be surprised . . . if from one side or the other, we have a very considerable storm to conquer. However, we have the right on our side—and that is the comfort.'[3]

Condemnation in the lawcourts was not enough to shake this conviction. In 1872 when the Privy Council declared vestments, wafer bread, the eastward position, and the mixed chalice illegal, one ritualist informed the Bishop of Oxford, 'I *cannot* make myself believe that the judgment of any court on earth can possibly override the faith of the universal Church.'[4] It was more difficult to counter the opposition of bishops, who might themselves claim to be an essential part of the universal Church. But the ritualists looked to the example of the Tractarians, who had already coped with episcopal

[1] Cf. the relationship between Lady Maria West and her ritualist son, in S. L. Ollard, *The Anglo-Catholic Revival*, 1925, p. 73.

[2] J. A. Froude, 'The Oxford Counter-Reformation' (1881) in *Short Studies on Great Subjects*, new edn., 1893, iv. 251. F. G. Lee, *The Need of Spiritual Authority, a Sermon*, 1882, p. 10.

[3] Louth, *The Influence of John Mason Neale*, p. 143.

[4] S. Meacham, *Lord Bishop, the Life of Samuel Wilberforce, 1805–1873*, Cambridge, Mass., 1970, p. 300.

criticism. 'It is everyone's duty to maintain Catholic truth,' Dr. Pusey told John Keble in 1842, 'even if unhappily opposed by a Bishop.' At the beginning of the 1870s, the ritualist Vicar of St. James's, Hatcham, refused even to discuss his practices with his diocesan bishop.[1] In the end the ritualists developed a technique of deciding for themselves when a bishop was behaving as a bishop and when he was not. As a sympathetic historian of the movement put it, if a bishop attempted to prohibit what they were doing, they 'knew he would not be acting as a bishop of the Catholic Church, but that he would be doing so either from the Erastian standpoint, or as exercising the expression of his own private judgement'.[2]

The Sources of Ritualism

In one respect ritualism merely reflected the general ornateness and 'conspicuous waste' of Victorian middle-class life. Gladstone noted that the amount of newly made wealth in the country encouraged ritual; he added that the preference of the rich for ornate churches and clergymen 'may represent not the spiritual growth, but the materializing tendencies of the age'. At the end of the century, the American sociologist Thornstein Veblen connected ritualism with the desire of a leisure class 'for the consumption of goods, material and immaterial'.[3] Influences of this kind, rather than doctrinal considerations, were presumably responsible for the ritualism which Gladstone professed to find among Nonconformists and that which Scotsmen saw 'infecting even our Presbyterian Churches'.[4]

Theologically, the movement developed out of Tractarianism. Some Tractarians, however, sought to distinguish the new movement rather sharply from the old. Dr. Pusey said that in the early Tractarian days there was 'a contemporary movement as to a very moderate ritual in a London congregation. We were united in friendship, but the movements were unconnected with each other.'[5] Pusey's memory was

[1] Liddon, *Life of Pusey*, ii. 238. Marsh, *The Victorian Church in Decline*, p. 127.
[2] J. Embry, *The Catholic Movement and the S.S.C.*, 1931, p. 200.
[3] Gladstone in the *Contemporary Review*, Oct. 1874, p. 677. T. Veblen, *The Theory of the Leisure Class* (1899), Unwin edn., 1970, p. 239.
[4] W. E. Gladstone, *The Church of England and Ritualism*, 1875, p. 24. *Dundee Advertiser*, 9 Oct. 1874.
[5] E. B. Pusey, *The Proposed Ecclesiastical Legislation*, 1874, p. 35.

faulty. As early as 1839 Newman had written to H. E. Manning, 'Give us more services, more vestments and decorations in worship.'[1] A movement that from the start looked for inspiration to church history, as the Tractarians did, was bound to bring about liturgical change. The real question was not whether the movement had stimulated ritual, but what sort of ritual was acceptable. Newman told Henry Wilberforce in 1849, 'When you propose to return to *lost* Church of England ways you are rational, but when you invent *new* ceremonial which never was, when you copy Roman or other foreign rituals, you are neither respectable nor rational.'[2]

Respectable and rational or not, Oxford remained a source of ritualist inspiration, protected by its sympathetic diocesan bishop, Samuel Wilberforce. In 1859 two ladies passed under the great window of Merton College Chapel and heard such sweet music that they went inside, where they were shocked by the sight of 'a regular Sister of Mercy, with a black cloth cloak and veil arranged over a great bonnet'.[3] The Chaplain, the Revd. H. M. Sargant, had introduced a weekly 'Choral Communion' with a surpliced choir whose fame had reached East Brent in Somerset by the early 1860s.[4] The Fellows of the college included High Churchmen like Edmund Hobhouse, who was Mackonochie's spiritual director, William Kerr Hamilton, the first High Churchman to be made a bishop, and R. J. Wilson, who became Warden of Keble. The influence of such men gave substance to the assertion of the *Liverpool Mercury* that ritualism was a 'religious fanaticism which is generally picked up at the University of Oxford'.[5]

None the less, as the daughter of Dean Church observed, Tractarianism as a distinctively Oxford enterprise was at an end and fresh developments were taking place elsewhere. Ritualism was also seen to be spreading from London.[6] The huge growth in the population of the capital made it an obvious place to build ritualist churches. St. Alban's, Holborn, St. Peter's, London Docks, St. Mary Magdalene's, Paddington,

[1] E. S. Purcell, *Life of H. E. Cardinal Manning*, 1896, i. 233.
[2] W. Ward, *Life of John Henry Cardinal Newman*, 1912, pp. 236 f.
[3] A. R. Mills, *Two Victorian Ladies*, 1969, p. 9.
[4] H. P. Denison, *Seventy-two Years' Church Recollections*, 1925, p. 32.
[5] *Liverpool Mercury*, 14 May 1874, p. 6.
[6] Church, *Life and Letters of Dean Church*, p. 61. *Quarterly Review*, Oct. 1874, p. 342.

and especially All Saints', Margaret Street, began to set new fashions in worship and ornateness.[1]

But the most important source of ritual innovation was undoubtedly Trinity College, Cambridge. The largest Cambridge college at this time,[2] it was the home of the Cambridge Camden Society, founded by Neale and Webb, as already noted, when they were undergraduates there. Their tutor, the Revd. Thomas Thorp (who later became Senior Tutor of the college) was one of thirteen Tractarians who signed a series of resolutions attacking the notorious Gorham judgement of 1850,[3] and he agreed to be president of the society. In 1843 Neale and Webb published, and dedicated to the Camden Society, their translation of *The Symbolism of Churches and Church Ornaments* by William Durandus. The society had begun to issue its magazine, *The Ecclesiologist*, two years previously. Initially the magazine concerned itself chiefly with church architecture, but at the eighth anniversary meeting in 1847 the society announced that its scope 'legitimately included' ritual. The following year it published the first of five volumes of *Hierurgia Anglicana*, announcing in the preface the intention of trying to restore daily prayers, weekly communion (at least), vestments, lighted and vested altars, etc., in the Church of England.[4]

By this time the society had moved its headquarters to London, where it survived as the Ecclesiological Society until 1863. But Trinity continued to produce ritualists. Two of the five priests to be imprisoned for ritualism, S. F. Green and Arthur Tooth, were Trinity men. So was Green's ritualist vicar at St. Peter's, Swinton, and his fellow curate there. Other notable Trinity ritualists were Knox-Little, Vicar of St. Alban's, Manchester, F. L. Bagshawe, who became master of the ritualist Society of the Holy Cross, J. R. A. Chinnery-Haldane, the Bishop of Argyll and the Isles, and W. J. Butler, Vicar of Wantage, where Mackonochie was curate.

---

[1] P. F. Anson, *Fashions in Church Furnishings*, 1960, p. 204.

[2] In 1841 Trinity admitted 135 students out of the 430 coming up; in 1851 the numbers were 148 out of 445: R. Robson, *Ideas and Institutions of Victorian Britain*, 1967, p. 322 and n. 2.

[3] *The Times*, 20 Mar. 1850.

[4] J. E. White, *The Cambridge Movement*, 1962, p. 205; cf. E. J. A. Boyce, *A Memorial of the Cambridge Camden Society*, 1888. *Hierurgia Anglicana*, 1848, p. v.

The limited ritual of the early Tractarians no longer sufficed the innovators. Many of them were now clearly imitating the Church of Rome, and the more intelligent admitted this. 'If the English Church be a true portion of the one Catholic Church of Christ,' argued R. W. Enraght, 'is it not only reasonable that her Church buildings and services should resemble those of other branches of the Church Catholic?' Such correspondences were extremely desirable, said the Revd. W. J. E. Bennett, for 'if Catholic England as represented by her national Church, could but be in union with Catholic Europe, then the great strong-holds of the enemy of souls in Heathen Lands would at last find their conqueror.' Inspired by Rome, he had already added stations of the cross to his church at Frome by the early 1860s.[1]

Many other examples of Roman Catholic influence can be traced. The Revd. C. F. Lowder took the lead in founding the Society of the Holy Cross (*Societas Sanctae Crucis*) in 1855 under the inspiration of St. Vincent de Paul, a copy of whose life he had found while staying at a Catholic school near Rouen. Other ritualists, led by the Revd. James Twigg of St. James's, Wednesbury, took up the example of the French missions. One of Twigg's curates, Charles Bodington, became Canon Missioner of the Lichfield diocese; another, George Body, became Canon Missioner in the Durham diocese.[2] The revival of Anglican Sisterhoods was a direct imitation of Roman Catholicism, contemporary prejudice against which meant that many Anglicans were shocked by such ritualist innovations. A senior clergyman in the Oxford diocese described the new Sisterhoods, along with the other ritualist activities, as part of an attempt 'to bring the Church of England to Rome by the furtive introduction . . . of Romish practices and observances'.[3]

Fear of Rome was still strong in Britain. In the 1870s, a Sussex antiquarian recorded the following dialect sentence: 'if so be as de Romans gets de upper hand an us, we shall be

[1] R. W. Enraght, *Catholic Worship*, 1871, p. 15. W. J. E. Bennett, *The Old Church Porch*, 1862, iv. 446. N. Pevsner, *North Somerset and Bristol*, 1958, pp. 195 f.

[2] J. F. Ede, *History of Wednesbury*, Birmingham, 1962, p. 312; on Bodington and Twigg see also D. Voll, *Catholic Evangelicalism*, trans. V. Ruffer, 1963, esp. pp. 50–3 and 74–8.

[3] *Facts and Documents shewing the Alarming State of the Diocese of Oxford*, by a Senior Clergyman of the Diocese, 1859, pp. 23–5 and 8.

Fig. 2

'Sliding on thin Ice.' Ritualists of the Church of England tempted to imitate the dangerous behaviour of Pius IX, Manning, and other Roman Catholic Clergymen.

burnded and bloodshedded, and have our Bibles took away from us.'[1] Some of the ritualists grew anxious to avoid the charge of romanizing. One of them explained that 'The usages you please to ticket as Romish are no more Romish than Oriental, no more Oriental than Russian, no more Russian than Jacobite, and no more Jacobite than Lutheran.'[2]

It was not true, and most Englishmen knew this. Their conviction was reinforced by the steady trickle of converts from ritualism to Rome. Some of those that stayed in the Church of England were less than loyal to it. Mackonochie used to put 'our Holy Mother the Church of England' at the top of his list when praying for the sick. The Revd. Joseph Leycester Lyne (Fr. Ignatius) at the age of twenty-nine visited a Roman Catholic priory, which inspired him to found an Anglican Benedictine monastery (with himself as superior); he had no qualms about having a Roman Catholic priest celebrate daily mass there.[3] Small wonder that many Protestants agreed with the Roman Catholic Bishop of Salford, Herbert Vaughan, when in 1874 he described the ritualists 'as Roman Catholics in all but their acknowledgement of the supremacy of Peter'.[4]

Auricular Confession

One issue aroused far greater opposition than any of the Six Points or illegal church ornament: the ritualists' advocacy of auricular confession. Pusey had revived the practice in the Church of England in 1838, and almost immediately people began to object. Bishop Blomfield described it as 'the source of unspeakable abominations'. Tait, as Bishop of London, withdrew a curate's licence for advocating it. In 1865 the Revd. A. D. Wagner was brutally assaulted in the streets of Brighton after newspaper reports that he had refused in court to answer questions that would 'involve him in a breach of the confessional'.[5]

---

[1] W. D. Parish, *A Dictionary of the Sussex Dialect*, Lewes, 1875, p. 62.

[2] B. M. P., *Lord Selborne's Letter to the 'Times' and an Answer*, by a Layman, 1874, p. 12.

[3] Reynolds, *Martyr of Ritualism*, p. 102. A. Calder-Marshall, *The Enthusiast*, 1962, pp. 77 and 154.

[4] *Eddows's Shrewsbury Journal*, 29 July 1874.

[5] C. J. Blomfield, *A Charge to the Clergy of London*, 1842, p. 30. Davidson and Benham, *Life of Tait*, i. 223 ff. E. W. Gilbert, *Brighton*, 1954, pp. 203 f.

None of this opposition discouraged the ritualists. G. R. Prynne openly defended confession in a pamphlet of 1852, and others followed suit. The priests at St. Alban's, Holborn, began by hearing confessions only in the vestry, but after 1859 they boldly started hearing them in the open church.[1] The Revd. Orby Shipley edited a volume of essays, two of which dealt with the subject. The first suggested that in some cases confession might be actually obligatory for Anglicans. The second urged its great value in preventing crimes against property and promoting chastity, and then went on to regret that few clergymen in the Church of England were properly qualified to hear people confess.[2] The ritualists took this last point extremely seriously, and in so doing reaped obloquy. In 1873 the Society of the Holy Cross presented a petition from 483 clergymen asking Convocation to consider providing 'for the education, selection, and licensing of duly qualified confessors in accordance with the provisions of Canon Law'. The petition, Pusey thought, was 'ill-advised'. Archbishop Tait called it 'evil'.[3] It caused an uproar.

Protestants objected to auricular confession first as a 'Romanizing Novelty' and 'one of the worst' of its kind.[4] Secondly, it was seen as an intrusion into Victorian family life. Bishop Wilberforce deplored it for superseding 'God's appointment of intimacy between husband and wife, father and children'. According to Archbishop Thomson, it exposed 'the sacredness of the hearth to a prying and often morbid curiosity'. These men were concerned above all to prevent prying curiosity about their womenfolk. 'I will suppress my own feelings,' said Canon Stowell of Salford, 'though they are ready to boil over; and I will not stir up the feelings of others, though I am sure the honest feelings of every Englishman, of every father, of every brother, of every husband, are startled when he thinks of the sister, the wife, the daughter, or the mother going into

[1] G. R. Prynne, *Private Confession, Penance, and Absolution authoritatively taught in the Church of England*, 1852; cf. J. H. Blunt, *Directorium Pastorale*, 1864. Reynolds, *Martyr of Ritualism*, pp. 183 f.

[2] *The Church and the World 1867*, 2nd edn., ed. O. Shipley, 1868, pp. 222, 387 ff., and 392.

[3] Pusey, *The Proposed Ecclesiastical Legislation*, p. 39. Tait in *Chronicle of Convocation*, 1873, p. 387.

[4] *Quarterly Review*, Oct. 1874, p. 107. Archdeacon Honey of Sarum in *Salisbury and Winchester Journal*, 23 May 1874.

"A WOLF IN SHEEP'S CLOTHING."

MR. BULL (*to* BRITANNIA). "WHENEVER YOU SEE ANY OF THESE SNEAKING SCOUNDRELS ABOUT, MA'AM
JUST SEND FOR ME. *I'LL DEAL WITH 'EM, NEVER FEAR!!*"

FIG. 3

John Bull protects British Womanhood from a ritualist priest wishing to
hear her confession.

the dark den of the confessional'.[1] Now the ritualists were asking for official sanction of this 'dark den'. 'No-one knows', said the *Quarterly Review*, 'how soon his sisters, daughters, or even his wife, or his sons, may yield to the persuasions of some friend or some clergyman whom they hold in high respect.'[2] The dispute involved a power-conflict between the Victorian paterfamilias and the ritualist clergyman. A similar phenomenon has been observed in present-day Latin America where, as a result of the close connection between women and the Roman Catholic church, the priesthood is said to have evolved for itself 'a competitive role *vis-à-vis* the family unit, and in so doing has diluted the control that male members are expected to exercise over their women'.[3]

Most of all, however, the Victorians deplored the confessional because, in the words of Bishop Wilberforce, it necessitated 'the terrible evil of familiar dealing with Sin, especially the sins of uncleanness'. Whereas other Roman Catholic practices were condemned only when brought into the Church of England, auricular confession aroused hostility of this kind wherever it was found. Referring to Roman Catholics, the Vicar of Harrogate said that common modesty prevented his quoting, 'even *in Latin*, the obscene, filthy interrogatories which are put, especially to females'. For over a century the leading English law case on obscenity was one which had arisen from an order, by Wolverhampton magistrates, for the destruction of a tract allegedly exposing Roman Catholic publications on the confessional.[4] The prurience surrounding this subject is explicable only in the context of the Victorian understanding of sexuality. First, it was believed that to excite sexual passion in women could lead to infertility: 'It is well known', declared a standard medical authority, 'that complaisance, tranquillity, silence, and secrecy, are necessary for prolific coition.'[5] The confessional, it was feared, would destroy the tranquillity as

[1] Wilberforce in J. W. Burgon, *Lives of Twelve Good Men*, 1888, ii. 56. H. K. Smith, *William Thomson, Archbishop of York*, 1958, p. 33. T. A. Stowell, *Lecture on Confession, delivered in the Free Trade Hall, Manchester*, Manchester, 1858, p. 1.

[2] *Quarterly Review*, Jan. 1874, p. 105.

[3] N. Yousseff, 'Cultural Ideals, Feminine Behaviour and Family Control', in *Comparative Studies in Science and History*, vol. 15, no. 3, June 1973, p. 342.

[4] Burgon, loc. cit.; George Digby, *A Brief Address*, Harrogate, 1842, p. 4; H. Street, *Freedom, the Individual and the Law*, 3rd edn., 1972, p. 120.

[5] M. Ryan, *The Philosophy of Marriage*, 1839, p. 260.

well as the secrecy. Secondly, many Victorian men treated their
wives in a fashion they preferred to keep to themselves rather
than have revealed to a clergyman. As Queen Victoria wrote
to her eldest daughter, 'men are very selfish and woman's
devotion is always one of submission, which makes our poor
sex so very unenviable. This you will feel hereafter—I know;
though it cannot be otherwise, as God has willed it so.'[1]

Aware of the danger of stirring up controversy in such a
delicate area, some ritualists now tried to keep their advocacy
of auricular confession as quiet as possible. In 1866 the first
half of *The Priest in Absolution*, by the Revd. J. C. Chambers,
was published openly; in 1870 the second half was circulated
secretly. (One ritualist wanted it published in Latin!) This was
to no avail, for the book was discovered and passages quoted
from it in the House of Lords. Mackonochie complained that
the extracts gave the impression that priests only asked about
purity and ignored the Ten Commandments.[2] As Parliament
prepared itself to legislate against the ritualists in 1874, their
opponents were similarly selective in attacking confession. At
a public meeting Lord Shaftesbury gave 'startling descriptions'
of what supposedly occurred in the confessional, drawn from
a work by Michelet called *Priests, Women, and Families*. In a
letter to *The Times*, Sir William Harcourt combined two objections to confession—fear of Rome, and hatred of any intrusion into family life—by quoting the boast of a confessor
who told the King of Spain, 'I hold your God in my hand,
and I have your wife at my feet.' All the 'paraphernalia of
Ritualistic practice and doctrine', said Harcourt, were designed
'to lead the way up to a similar pretension'.[3]

In the face of this hostility, some tried to defend confession
by appealing to Anglican authorities such as Hooker, Bishop
Jewel, and parts of the Prayer Book;[4] but none of these were
relevant to the real grounds on which men objected to the
practice. One of the few ritualists to try to fight the objectors

---

[1] *Dearest Child, Letters between Queen Victoria and the Princess Royal, 1858–1861*,
ed. R. Fulford, 1964, p. 44.

[2] Reynolds, op. cit., p. 213, for the Latin advocate. A. H. Mackonochie,
'*The Priest in Absolution*' *and the Society of the Holy Cross*, 1877, p. 17.

[3] Hodder, *Life of Shaftesbury*, p. 679. *The Times*, 30 July 1874.

[4] T. T. Carter, *The Freedom of Confession in the Church of England*, 1872. E. B.
Pusey, *Habitual Confession*, 1877.

on their own ground in 1874 was the Revd. C. F. Lowder. He pointed out that women naturally frequented the confessional more than men because they had always shown more devotion to Christ. None the less, he asserted, to use the confessional demanded more courage than to defend a wicket against a fast bowler, charge an awkward fence when hunting, or volunteer for the Ashanti War. Finally, he asked the Bishop of London whether he had ever realized as a schoolmaster the extent to which sins of impurity prevailed amongst boys: 'There are sins which most of all required nipping in the bud, which a boy would never dream of mentioning to his parent, though he would readily confess them to a sympathizing priest.'[1]

Lowder's defence came too late. Auricular confession was now arousing greater hostility than ever before, and action was being demanded against its advocates. In 1868 the *Quarterly Review* had attacked the practice. Now it returned to the attack with greater virulence, declaring that this 'special aspect of the Ritualist movement has become even more serious than ever'.[2] It was surely now time to put down the ritualists, men felt, if only for the sake of decency.

The Opposition

The significance of the ritualists' activities was not always immediately apparent. Even Pusey once confessed that for some time he had no idea that the eastward position meant anything special at the Eucharist. Opponents of the ritualists, such as Bishop Magee of Peterborough and Bishop Fraser of Manchester, had no objection to it. At the end of 1874 the Evangelical Edward Bickersteth told Archbishop Tait that the feeling in many parts was 'very strong in favour of making it an open position'.[3]

What made it far from optional to ritualists was its doctrinal significance. The eastward position, wrote Charles Walker, 'is the position of a Sacrificing priest'. Mackonochie believed that a 'gorgeously conducted service' showed that at the

---

[1] C. F. Lowder, *Sacramental Confession examined by Pastoral Experience*, 1874, pp. 34, 16, and 28 f.

[2] *Quarterly Review*, Jan. 1874, p. 105; cf. *Quarterly Review*, Jan. 1868, pp. 83–116.

[3] Liddon, *Life of Pusey*, iv. 210 f. MacDonnell, *Life of Magee*, ii. 69. J. W. Diggle, *The Lancashire Life of Bishop Fraser*, 1899, p. 160. Bickersteth to Tait, Tait Papers, Misc. Corr. and P.W.R.A., fos. 337 ff.

Eucharist Christ's body and blood were really present under the form of bread and wine.[1] As such doctrinal implications became clear, toleration ceased. The notion of the Eucharistic Sacrifice was anathema to most Protestants; one of the Thirty-nine Articles had condemned the 'sacrifices of Masses' as 'blasphemous fables, and dangerous deceits'. In 1882 the Evangelical theologian, Handley Moule, wrote that the 'Holy Supper' was 'an occasion for our noblest spiritual sacrifices; but that is altogether another thing from its being itself a sacrifice.'[2] The ritualists made use of new hymnals (which were appearing in the middle of the century at a rate of rather more than one a year)[3] to import into their worship doctrines hardly hinted at in the Prayer Book. As a result, Anglicans who might have been enjoying a certain ornateness in a ritualist church suddenly found themselves singing doctrines they detested. This happened, in 1874 and 1875, to the Dean of Durham and the former Bishop of St. David's, Connop Thirlwall. Both wrote complaining to Archbishop Tait.[4]

Every success in the introduction of ritual, said the Dean of Canterbury in 1863, was 'a step in the deterioration of the national character', and others agreed.[5] Two methods of stopping this were available. One group of Protestants saw the solution in a revision of the Prayer Book. Lord Ebury, a prominent Evangelical peer, led the small but wealthy Prayer Book Revision Society. In 1860 he failed to persuade Parliament to set up a royal commission with the object of revising the Prayer Book in a more Protestant direction.[6] Ebury was aware that the ritualists could appeal 'confidently' and 'not altogether unsuccessfully' to the Prayer Book in confirmation of their doctrines.[7] But other Protestants maintained that a proper inter-

---

[1] C. Walker, *The Ritual Reason Why*, 1866, p. 133. Mackonochie in Reynolds, *Martyr of Ritualism*, p. 109.

[2] H. C. G. Moule, *The Supper of the Lord*, 1882, p. 49.

[3] R. C. D. Jasper, 'The Prayer Book in the Victorian Era' in *The Victorian Crisis of Faith*, ed. A. Symondson, 1970, p. 114.

[4] Tait Papers, Misc. Corr., vol. 193, fos. 338 f. Davidson and Benham, *Life of Tait*, ii. 310.

[5] e.g. J. T. Tomlinson, who quoted the Dean in *The Literary Morality of the Ritualists*, 1867, p. 8.

[6] Lord Ebury, *Notes on the Declaration against a Revision of the Prayer-Book*, 2nd edn., 1860.

[7] Lord Ebury, *On the Revision of the Liturgy*, 1860, p. 11. Cf. *Romanizing Germs: are there any in the Prayer Book*, by a Clergyman, the Prayer-Book Revision Society, 1874.

pretation of the Ornaments Rubric showed that the Church of England had 'never retained any of the vestments or instruments of the mass', although in fact the ambiguities of the Elizabethan settlement made the Prayer Book a valuable weapon for defending ritualist practices.[1] And in so far as Evangelicals urged a revision of the Prayer Book they appeared to be tacitly conceding the ritualists' case. Ebury failed to get through a revision even of the burial service. In 1867, when Lord Shaftesbury brought in a bill to amend the Rubric by giving the force of the law to Canon Fifty-eight, he found himself opposed by a majority in the Lords including seven bishops.

Tait, however, and eleven other bishops voted with Shaftesbury. These men believed that the right way to deal with the ritualists was through the courts. If the Prayer Book was ambiguous, the law would soon make matters clear. This notion was enthusiastically supported by a group of Evangelicals who in 1865 had formed the Church Association with the express purpose of stopping the ritualists by prosecuting them. (Its first report said that a revision of the Prayer Book was not part of its plans.[2]) By 1869 the Association had over 7,000 members, including among its vice-presidents many Irish peers and half a dozen Members of Parliament. Even some professed opponents of the ritualists found the Church Association unduly virulent. Bishop Fraser called it a persecution association,[3] a name he also applied to the High Church and ritualist English Church Union. The E.C.U. had, in fact, been the first to have recourse to the law, attempting to prosecute the Evangelical Bishop of Carlisle for heresy in 1862.[4]

The Church Association's first important attempts to prosecute were successful. On its behalf, Martin prosecuted Mackonochie in 1867 for using altar lights, kneeling during the consecration, elevating the eucharistic elements, mixing water

---

[1] M. McColl, *The Advertisements of 1564, Fresh Evidence against the Purchas Judgement*, 1875, *passim*.

[2] C. H. H. Wright and C. Neil, *A Protestant Dictionary*, 1904, p. 108.

[3] At the Stockport Church Institute Annual Soiree, Nov. 1874, reported *Stockport Advertiser*, 27 Nov. 1874, p. 7. Bishop Magee is usually given credit for this nickname, as in G. W. E. Russell, *Edward King, Sixtieth Bishop of Lincoln*, 1912, p. 146.

[4] L. E. Elliott-Binns, *Religion in the Victorian Era*, 2nd edn., 1964, p. 235.

THE CHICHESTER EXTINGUISHER.

Bishop of Chichester. "GO! GO! YOU INSOLENT, REBELLIOUS BOY. WHAT WITH YOUR NONSENSE AND INCENSE AND CANDLES YOU'LL BE SETTING THE CHURCH ON FIRE."

Master P-ch-s. "JUST WHAT I'D LIKE TO DO. THERE!"

FIG. 4

Bishop Gilbert of Chichester attacks the Revd. John Purchas for using incense and altar candles.

and wine in the chalice, and using incense. The Dean of Arches, Sir Robert Phillimore, said that the first three were lawful; but Martin appealed to the Judicial Committee of the Privy Council, which condemned Mackonochie on all points. When he refused to comply with the judgement, he was suspended for three months. The Church Association immediately instituted the prosecution of the Revd. John Purchas, Vicar of St. James's, Brighton, and again the Privy Council found against him, this time concerning thirty-three points which included vestments and the eastward position. Again, the ruling of the Dean of Arches was reversed.

'By degrees', observed Bishop Fraser, 'the meaning of certain ambiguous rubrics in the Book of Common Prayer have become plainer in consequence of the interpretations which have been placed upon them by the Court of Final Appeal.'[1] No one, however, was satisfied. For one thing, the ritualists simply ignored what the Privy Council had decided. For another, the cases lasted too long. (The Purchas case took three years; Mackonochie's took four, and involved five hearings altogether.) What the Church needed, said Tait, was a 'summary process for the present system of protracted legislation'. As he pointed out, litigation cost money; and even if the Church Association had plenty, others (including bishops) did not. The Purchas case, he told Parliament, ran up costs of £7,661, and an earlier unsuccessful attempt to convict the Revd. W. J. E. Bennett of Romish heresy had cost altogether £11,015.[2]

Moreover, the extreme behaviour of some ritualists was now alienating some of the High Churchmen who once supported them. Lewis Carroll said that although he 'naturally' adopted the High Church views of his father, he 'felt repelled' by ritualism. Bishop Wilberforce told the Revd. J. L. Lyne that his pseudo-Benedictine habit was 'a sacrifice of the kernel to the shell such as I have never seen equalled'. What Bishop Magee called 'the line of demarcation between the sound and the gangrened parts of the High Church school' was becoming clearer.[3] In 1873 the Revd. J. W. Burgon preached against the

---

[1] Diggle, op. cit., p. 159.   [2] Hansard, vol. 218, 1874, 797 and 794.

[3] S. D. Collingwood, Life and Letters of Lewis Carroll, 2nd edn., n. d., p. 340. Calder-Marshall, The Enthusiast, p. 101.

ritualists in Oxford University Church. He said it was painful
to be forced into a position directly hostile to many of his friends;
but he had concluded that their pitiful millinery, their coloured
stoles, and imported birettas would undoubtedly 'betray many
unstable souls into the hand of the Church of Rome'.[1]

The call for new legislation against ritualists intensified. In
February 1874, the *Fortnightly Review* carried an article by
F. W. Newman asking the Commons to pass 'declaratory laws'
enabling parishioners to 'eject' them. A 'High Churchman of
the Old School' called it a 'national grievance' that bishops
could not stop the plague which might spread everywhere.
Eight Evangelical clergymen in Liverpool warned that disestablishment and disintegration would ensue unless something
were done to uphold constitutional authority in the Church.[2]

In May 1874, Judge Keating supported the Bishop of Exeter's
contention that the new reredos in his cathedral was illegal,
and ordered its demolition. The Dean and Chapter appealed
to the Privy Council. 'It is to be hoped that legislation will
shortly place the Ritualist and the Reredos thus far on the
same footing,' said *Punch*; 'that the former, if he persists in
performing illicit rites in his Church, shall be liable to be, if
not straightway demolished, at least summarily removed.'[3]

Disraeli, the Queen, and the Bishops

As Parliament contemplated legislation against the ritualists,
some members of both Houses were certain to support them.
A number of important Lords—Salisbury, Bath, Carnarvon—
were ritualists, along with less important ones like Beauchamp,
Devon, and Nelson. In the Commons, A. J. B. Beresford Hope
(a former President of the Ecclesiological Society), J. G.
Hubbard, A. E. Gathorne-Hardy, and above all Gladstone,
would also fight for them. But at the beginning of 1874 the
Liberals lost the general election and Disraeli became Prime
Minister.

Men still doubted Disraeli's sincerity. 'He cannot make up
his mind', said Lord Shaftesbury, 'whether to be Evangelical,

---

[1] J. W. Burgon, *Romanizing within the Church of England*, 1873, pp. 33 f.

[2] *Fortnightly Review*, new ser., vol. xv, Feb. 1874, p. 189. *Quosque? How Far?
How Long?* by a High Churchman of the Old School, 1873, pp. 10 f. *Daily Courier*,
20 Apr. 1874, p. 7.

[3] *Punch*, 16 May 1874.

Neologian, or Ritualistic; he is waiting for the highest bidder.'[1] Yet for the greater part of his political career Disraeli's religious opinions remained consistent. In 1868 he told both Archbishop Tait and Lord Derby that his church policy was to persuade Evangelicals and High Churchmen to combine against ritualists and rationalists.[2] What churchmen disliked was the way he regarded the Church as 'the great State-engine of the Conservatives' (to quote Dean Wellesley). They knew, as Magee said, that the Church would never weigh with him against the interests of his party.[3] He refused to prefer High Churchmen to the bench of bishops not because he was friendly with none of them but because, as he told Lord Stanley, he believed they were supported only by some dons, some youthful priests, and perhaps many women; and the last had no votes.[4] His religious stance was motivated by his political ambitions. In 1868 he had told Tait that he would support a 'Church Discipline Bill'. At that time he was convinced that 'the long pent-up feeling of this nation against ultra-ritualism' would ensure political success for any party that showed itself to be sufficiently Protestant.[5] But since he had lost the general election at the end of the year, there was no certainty that his plans for church discipline had survived from 1868 to 1874.

Disraeli had little time for the Archbishop, whom he regarded as 'obscure in purpose, fitful and inconsistent in action' and 'a prey to constantly conflicting convictions'. Since Tait was also a Liberal, he would never have reached Canterbury had the Queen not overridden Disraeli's objections.[6] Would Disraeli now respond to her hatred of the ritualists? Victoria was obsessed with the menace of Rome. The Protestant churches, she believed, must unite to constitute 'a strong phalanx, forgetting *small differences* of form in *the one great cause of Protestantism*'. She went so far as to tell the German Emperor that the 'essentially Protestant' English would inevitably sympathize with

---

[1] Hodder, *Life of Shaftesbury*, p. 631.
[2] W. F. Monypenny and G. E. Buckle, *Life of Disraeli*, new edn., 1929, ii. 408. Davidson and Benham, *Life of Tait*, i. 536.
[3] Wellesley, quoted in Blake, *Disraeli*, p. 507. MacDonnell, *Life of Magee*, ii. 2.
[4] Monypenny and Buckle, op. cit. ii. 400.
[5] Davidson and Benham, op. cit. i. 536. Ashwell and Wilberforce, *Life of Wilberforce*, iii. 267.
[6] *Letters of Queen Victoria*, i. 549.

him in any dispute with France—the Kaiser, not surprisingly, thought this 'a most fortunate circumstance'. Victoria, therefore, had no disposition to tolerate the innovators who by imitating 'Romish forms' were undermining 'the Protestant character' of the English Church. 'Something *must be done*', she told Archbishop Tait on 15 January 1874; the bishops should be given enhanced powers by legislation, and acting with lay support should take drastic measures against 'Romanizing tendencies'.[1]

Her proposals were entirely congenial to Tait, who made no secret of his belief that the ritualists' practices were 'tomfooleries' suitable only for 'an utter fool or madman'.[2] Samuel Wilberforce, the one bishop powerful enough to stand up to Tait in defence of the ritualists, had been killed in July 1873 by falling from his horse. Now, as the Bishop of Lincoln observed, Tait dominated the others. After the first bishops' meeting to discuss the Queen's proposals, the Archbishop himself made a note in his diary that all but two of them were younger than he was.[3] In any case most of them shared his dislike of the ritualists. The bench still reflected the patronage of Lord Palmerston, who never made an episcopal appointment without consulting the extreme Evangelical Lord Shaftesbury. Palmerston's policy meant that apart from Harold Browne, to whom he gave the bishopric of Ely, none of his bishops was remotely sympathetic to Tractarians, let alone ritualists.[4]

Many had already made their attitude abundantly clear. Archbishop Thomson of York refused permission for ritualist missions, never ordained a ritualist, and would revoke the licences of ritualist curates. C. T. Baring of Durham, who considered ritualist ways and beliefs to be 'parasitic weeds' which sucked vitality from the church, refused to consecrate churches if the number of steps between the nave and the altar exceeded three and thus perhaps hinted at ritualist symbolism. Pelham of Norwich, in his visitation charge of 1872, attacked the ritual-

---

[1] *Letters of Queen Victoria*, ii. 314 and 327. Ponsonby, *Henry Ponsonby*, p. 177. Tait Papers, Notebook 52, 11 Jan. 1874; and *Letters of Queen Victoria*, ii. 300.
[2] Davidson and Benham, op. cit. i. 232 f.
[3] E. W. Watson, *Life of Bishop John Wordsworth*, 1915, p. 99. Tait Papers, Notebook 52, 17 Jan. 1874.
[4] Hodder, op. cit., p. 609; and J. Ridley, *Lord Palmerston*, Panther edn., 1972, pp. 670 ff.

ists for teaching the Eucharistic Sacrifice and the Real Presence. Philpott of Worcester believed they were 'undoing the Reformation' and that an act of Parliament to prevent this was undoubtedly needed.[1] Non-Palmerstonian bishops joined in. Joshua Hughes of St. Asaph refused priest's orders to a curate who followed his vicar's custom and used the eastward position. Lord Arthur Charles Hervey of Bath and Wells said that the ritualists were as fanatical as the Indian mutineers and the Scottish covenanters.[2]

Even the attitude of Harold Browne was not clearly on the side of tolerance. He had been commended to Victoria on the grounds that his learning and wisdom pleased 'even those who would naturally be most afraid of his supposed High Church views'. As a parish priest in Exeter he had appeared in church wearing a surplice and then hurriedly resigned, leaving his successor to bear the brunt of the uproar! Gladstone had made him Bishop of Winchester in 1873. Now, at the beginning of 1874, Victoria rightly or wrongly asserted that he too was alarmed at the state of the Church.[3]

Disraeli himself had put on the episcopal bench two men who were to play markedly different roles in the forthcoming legislation. Under pressure from the Queen[4] he had reluctantly sent Magee to Peterborough in 1868. Magee was sympathetic to High Churchmen and greatly disliked the Calvinism of some of the Low Churchmen. But he was an Irish Protestant: he hated romanizers; and he described the ritualists as very spoilt children, 'scratching and biting their elderly kindly nurses (the bishops)' and trying to kick over the supper table because they could not have the cloth and dishes set out exactly as they liked.[5] He was determined to put them down.

Equally determined to support them was Christopher Wordsworth, whom Disraeli had sent to Lincoln in 1868 as a shining example of how 'a true Protestant may be a sound

[1] H. K. Smith, *William Thomson*, pp. 41 f. J. B. Dykes, *Eucharistic Truth*, 1874, p. 61; and C. T. Baring, *A Charge to the Clergy*, 1878, p. 29. J. T. Pelham, *A Charge to the Clergy*, 1872, p. 30. H. Philpott, *A Charge to the Clergy*, 1877, pp. 14 and 21.

[2] *Eddows's Shrewsbury Journal*, 10 June 1874, pp. 5 and 7. *Western Gazette*, 16 Oct. 1874, p. 3.

[3] G. W. Kitchin, *E. H. Browne*, 1895, p. 73. *Letters of Queen Victoria*, iii. 372, and ii. 302.

[4] Monypenny and Buckle, op. cit. ii. 406 f.

[5] MacDonnell, op. cit. i. 82 f., and ii. 101.

Churchman'.[1] The Prime Minister had perhaps been misled by Wordsworth's activities in 1866, when he led a deputation to Archbishop Longley claiming that ritualist innovations were 'stumbling blocks in the way of souls for whom Christ died'.[2] Wordsworth had attacked these innovations in Convocation; but in 1874 he told a friend that the Erastian nature of the proposed new legislation made the Church appear nothing more than a tool of the State and would surely drive many clergymen to Rome. He publicly attacked as unconstitutional the idea that Parliament could legislate for the Church without the help of Convocation, and announced his fear of schism if the proposed bill became law.[3] Throughout 1874 he worked tirelessly to frustrate Tait's intentions.

He was supported in this by three bishops appointed by Gladstone. Harvey Goodwin, who replaced the Evangelical Waldegrave of Carlisle in 1869, believed something should be done to curb excess, but he was quite sure that the Archbishop's proposals were the wrong remedy. George Moberly of Salisbury, in his visitation charge of 1873, had gone so far as to praise ornateness in worship (provided all were done legally). Both he and Goodwin refused to be panicked over auricular confession, and Moberly actually described it as 'holy and good'.[4] The third bishop was J. F. Mackarness of Oxford, who had been one of the coterie of ritualists and High Churchmen based on Merton. As early as the so-called Papal Aggression of 1850 he had stood out against the 'no popery' cry.[5] Now he declared that politicians had always sacrificed ecclesiastical interests to their own ends. He warned Anglicans that the declaration of Papal infallibility showed what happened to religious men who were after too much power![6]

Tait deplored what he called 'the spirit of insubordination'

[1] J. Overton and E. Wordsworth, *Christopher Wordsworth, Bishop of Lincoln*, 1888, pp. 203 f.

[2] *Guardian*, 7 Feb. 1866, p. 138.

[3] Overton and Wordsworth, op. cit., pp. 186 ff., and 264 f. C. Wordsworth, *States and Synods, their Respective Functions and Uses*, 1874, p. 16, and *A Plea for Toleration in certain Ritual Matters*, 1874, pp. 6 and 11.

[4] H. Goodwin in *Liverpool Mercury*, 28 Aug. 1874, p. 7. G. Moberly, *A Charge to the Clergy*, 1873, pp. 20, 29, and 37. H. Goodwin, *Confession*, 1873, p. 12.

[5] J. F. Mackarness, *A Plea for Toleration in answer to the No Popery Cry*, 1850.

[6] J. F. Mackarness, *A Charge delivered to the Diocese of Oxford*, Oxford, 1872, pp. 9 and 23.

among 'Gladstone's YOUNG MEN at the bottom of the table', who had not understood 'what their seniors had settled for them'.[1] Gladstone's appointments, however, were by no means all High Churchmen. He took far more care in this matter than did Disraeli. (His private secretary observed that a vacant see 'excited him far more than a political crisis'.[2]) He was concerned to keep a 'balance' on the bench and claimed that of his thirty episcopal appointments eleven were High Churchmen and nineteen were not.[3] None of his bishops, apart from the eleven High Churchmen, was likely to give much hope to the ritualists in 1874, though many thought Temple might leave them alone (which he did until he became Archbishop of Canterbury), and were not sure what to think about James Fraser. For a time Fraser had been strongly attracted to Puseyism. He had been chaplain to the High Church Bishop Hamilton of Salisbury. George Moberly had recommended that Gladstone appoint him to the see of Manchester.[4] But two weeks after his consecration, Fraser asserted that he had never belonged to any party in the Church and hoped never to join any. In 1872 he declared he desired to erect 'no narrow or Procrustean standard' for the clergy. Almost in the next breath he said that 'a reform of the church courts', as regards to their cost 'and also their cumbrous forms of procedure', appeared to be one of the most needful improvements of the day.[5] By 1874 he was backing the Archbishop.

[1] Quoted in D. W. R. Bahlman 'The Queen, Mr. Gladstone, and Church Patronage' in *Victorian Studies*, vol. iii, no. 4, 1960, p. 358.

[2] Ibid., p. 357.

[3] C. K. F. Brown, *A History of the English Clergy*, 1953, p. 123.

[4] J. Bryce, *Studies in Contemporary Biography*, 1903, p. 201.

[5] Diggle, *Life of Bishop Fraser*, p. 265. J. Fraser, *Charge delivered at his Primary Visitation*, Manchester, 1872, pp. 44 and 50.

III

THE PUBLIC WORSHIP
REGULATION ACT

The Archbishop's Preparations

To curb the ritualists, Tait needed the backing of both the Government and most of the bishops. He considered the support of the former more important, and had brought up a tentative scheme in the Lords the previous year without even consulting the bishops about it.[1] In 1874, assuming that Gladstone would remain Prime Minister, Tait made approaches to him on the subject through the Queen; but Gladstone prudently waited until Parliament was dissolved before sending a reply counselling caution.[2]

Not all the bishops saw Disraeli's victory in the ensuing election as a blessing. Magee, for instance, wrote that he was 'very doubtful still how far the Church is better or worse for the change'.[3] But Tait immediately wrote to Disraeli proposing a simple and inexpensive means of prosecuting ritualists. His aim was to increase the power of the bishops. They should be able either to ignore infringements of the law or to try them (advised by a board of clergymen and laymen). If an incumbent refused to accept his bishop's decision, Tait suggested that his benefice should be sequestrated.[4]

Tait had informed the bishops at their January meeting that the Queen wanted action against ritualism, adding that Parliament should be asked to legislate as soon as possible. Randall Davidson decided not to publish Tait's notes of this meeting, alleging that Moberly of Salisbury was 'the single Bishop who thought the introduction of such a measure undesirable'.[5] But the notes show that Mackarness of Oxford

---

[1] Hansard, 3rd Ser., vol. 217, 278. Tait put 'church discipline' on the agenda of the bishops' meeting in November 1873.

[2] *Letters of Queen Victoria*, ii. 300–2.   [3] MacDonnell, *Life of Magee*, i. 296.

[4] Beaconsfield Papers, B/XII/F/3, 24 Feb. 1874.

[5] Davidson and Benham, *Life of Tait*, ii. 190, and 228, n. 1.

also flatly opposed the idea of legislation, and that Wordsworth of Lincoln agreed with it only on the condition that Convocation would be consulted first. Tait brushed aside Wordsworth's suggestion that the bishops put out an address to churchmen on the subject. Then in March he astonished his colleagues by leaking a report of the intended bill through Delane of *The Times* without consulting any of them.[1]

In his negotiations with the Government, Tait showed none of this high-handedness. On 10 March he received a sarcastic letter from Disraeli: 'I conclude, by the article in the "Times" today, that you have a bill prepared. Is there any objection to my seeing it?'[2] The Archbishop (who had almost died of rheumatic fever in 1848 and remained a partial invalid since that time) was too ill to go out until 26 March, when he took the Prime Minister the draft bill which he himself had prepared with the assistance of J. D. Brunel, the Chancellor of Ely. It followed his earlier outline, except that appeals were now to be heard by the archbishops, and the penalty for disobedient clergymen was to be inhibition for up to three months, with the consequent loss of official income.[3]

Tait was perfectly willing to let the Government change his bill, and he had already written to Lord Cairns asking his advice.[4] Cairns was now for the second time Lord Chancellor. An Ulster Orangeman, and therefore a convinced Evangelical, he taught in Sunday-school to the end of his life, refusing to let his profession interfere with his religion. Rather the reverse: it was said that barristers not otherwise known for their piety but desirous of county court judgeships were sometimes seen at his prayer meetings,[5] and he was accused of improper interference in ritual cases.[6] But few disputed his ability. In 1861, one of the pupils introduced by Cairns into the Middle Temple observed that 'the reverend Masters put on their glasses and looked at me with a respect bordering on devotion'. Disraeli had turned urgently to Cairns for help in preparing the hasty

---

[1] Tait Papers, Notebook 52, 17 Jan. 1874; Misc. Corr. and P.W.R.A., vol. 193, letter to Delane 6 Mar. 1874; MacDonnell, op. cit. ii. 2–3.

[2] Tait Papers, Misc. Corr. and P.W.R.A., vol. 193, 10 Mar. 1974.

[3] B/XII/F/20.

[4] Cairns Papers, P.R.O. 30/51/15, 7 Mar. 1874.

[5] Bryce, *Studies in Contemporary Biography*, p. 194.

[6] G. W. E. Russell, *St. Alban the Martyr, a History of Fifty Years*, 1913, p. 81.

election manifesto of 1874.[1] Now he told the Prime Minister that he agreed with the Archbishop's intentions, but that the draft bill was bound to meet opposition in the Cabinet—not only from the High Churchmen but also from the Evangelicals, who were unlikely to give so much discretionary power to the bishops; in any case, the form in which Tait had submitted his proposals was crude and unworkable.[2]

Cairns was right about the Cabinet, which described the Archbishop's proposals as 'disastrous', although (as Disraeli hastened to assure the Queen) there was 'almost unanimity of opinion' that the Government should help him. Victoria had already told him that this was what she wanted, and he was concealing the true extent of the opposition.[3] Before accepting Cabinet office in 1874 Lord Salisbury had sought (and believed he had received) an assurance that the Government would neither introduce nor support a measure hostile to the ritualists. Gathorne-Hardy told Disraeli that it would be difficult to draw up a worse bill than the one proposed, and Lord Carnarvon said that Parliament would never grant the powers that the bishops were requesting.[4] To Lady Bradford the Prime Minister confided his fear that the matter would break up not only his ministry but even the Church of England itself; it was 'the hardest nut to crack that ever was the lot of a Minister'. Disraeli's solution was to ask the archbishops to force upon their colleagues a bill completely redrafted by Cairns. 'The plot thickens,' he wrote after meeting them, 'but I think I shall steer the ship safely.' On 17 April the bishops met for six hours and accepted Cairns's suggestions.[5]

Faced with a ritual case, they were now to be advised by a board drawn up according to the provisions of the Church Discipline Act of 1840; Parliament had already once agreed to these provisions and therefore might agree to them again. This would be provocative enough, but more serious was the

---

[1] D. Hudson, *Munby, Man of Two Worlds*, 1972, p. 105. *The Letters of Disraeli to Lady Bradford and Lady Chesterfield*, ed. the Marquess of Zetland, 1929, i. 49.
[2] Monypenny and Buckle, *Life of Disraeli*, ii. 659–60.
[3] *Letters of Queen Victoria*, ii. 332–3. Monypenny and Buckle, op. cit. ii. 658.
[4] Lady G. Cecil, *Life of Robert Marquis of Salisbury*, 1921, ii. 49–50. A. E. Gathorne-Hardy, *Gathorne-Hardy, First Earl of Cranbrook*, 1910, i. 338–40; MacDonnell, op. cit. ii. 2.
[5] Disraeli, *Letters*, i. 63 and 71.

suggestion that appeals were now to be made to the Judicial Committee of the Privy Council, since many High Churchmen considered it deficient in spiritual authority. The archbishops had found it difficult to convert all their colleagues to the new draft. They confessed to the Prime Minister that the High Church bishops, especially Moberly and Mackarness, were still opposed to any form of legislation. In reply Disraeli simply gave them an account of his own problems: there were High Churchmen and neutrals in the Cabinet, and the Queen was taking a 'female view' of the question.[1] Even now he could not pledge the Government's full support to the bill; as he told Tait on 13 April, 'all the Lord Chancellor, and myself, have done in this matter is as two sincere Churchmen and personal friends of your Grace'.[2]

Tait now had a bill never fully endorsed by the bishops and altered at the request of a government which refused to support it publicly. He had no intention of seeking the approval of anyone else before submitting his proposals to Parliament, even though the bishops had agreed in January to consult the clergy in Convocation and eight of them brought the matter up again at a meeting in March.[3] Unless Convocation were consulted, it was suggested, the clergy would 'complain that they were taken at unawares'. Convocation had been revived partly because Parliament, with the admission of Dissenters and Roman Catholics, no longer seemed to many to be a suitable body to legislate for the Church of England.[4] It was argued that if the clergy were consulted, they would be more willing to obey the bill when it had passed into law.

Tait disagreed, and others with him. A. P. Stanley believed that Convocation was such a hotbed of ritualists that it ought to be destroyed, not consulted. The *Edinburgh Review* said that once Convocation took over Parliament's powers of ecclesiastical legislation, the Church of England would become 'an Episcopal

---

[1] Tait Papers, Notebook 52, 19 and 25 Apr. 1874. Monypenny and Buckle, op. cit. ii. 660.

[2] Tait Papers, Misc. Corr. and P.W.R.A., vol. 193, 13 Apr. 1874.

[3] Ibid., 6 Mar. 1874, fos. 149 f. Harold Browne reported on this meeting to the Bishop of London, who sent his letter on to Tait.

[4] See E. W. Kemp, *Counsel and Consent*, 1961, especially lecture 7, 'Suppression and Revival'. P. Welch, 'The Revival of an Active Convocation of Canterbury (1852–1855)', *Journal of Ecclesiastical History*, vol. 10, 1959, pp. 188–97.

sect with a strong sacerdotal basis'.[1] Tait took advantage of
the fact that in 1874 Easter had delayed the reassembly of the
representatives of the clergy, and without consulting them he
went ahead. They met on 28 April, the day fixed for the second
reading of the bill in the House of Lords. The day before, two
High Church peers appealed to Tait to postpone the second
reading until 11 May. Tait argued against this, but gave in
when Cairns himself asked for a postponement. The Archbishop said he hoped it would be only for a few days.[2]

His distrust of the lower clergy in Convocation turned out
to be fully justified. In the Southern Province they unanimously
adopted a resolution of Lord Alwyne Compton regretting that
they were unable to approve of the bill. In the Northern
Province they rejected the Dean of Carlisle's amendment in
favour of the bill by twenty-three votes to fifteen. The clergy
reported that they disliked the way Tait was attempting to
discipline ceremonial when there were far more serious abuses
in the Church to be dealt with.[3] And, as the Dean of Windsor
said, they remained 'very sore' at not being consulted before the
bill was brought in.[4] Had Tait consulted them earlier they would
still have disagreed with his bill; by failing to do so he merely
gave them a further reason for objecting to it.

By revealing his proposals to *The Times*, Tait had provoked
a public outcry from the clergy. Dr. Pusey replied with three
long letters (immediately published 'by request' as a pamphlet),
urging that few were breaking the law and that in any case
the legality of many points at issue was very much in doubt.
He added that Parliament, with its quota of Dissenters and
unbelievers, was no fit body to legislate for the clergy, and that
a lay judge, with his lack of theological learning, was no fit
person to judge between them.[5] He suggested that if the eastward position were allowed the ritualists might voluntarily
abandon their other objectionable practices. This was naïve;
distrust of Parliament amongst Tractarians had developed into

[1] R. E. Prothero and G. G. Bradley, *Life and Correspondence of A. P. Stanley*,
3rd edn., 1894, ii. 214. *Edinburgh Review*, Oct. 1874, p. 451.
[2] Hansard, 2nd Ser., vol. 218, 1146–50. Davidson and Benham, op. cit., makes
no mention of this.
[3] *Chronicle of Convocation*, 1874, pp. 36 ff. *Liverpool Mercury*, 23 May 1874, p. 7.
[4] Tait Papers, Misc. Corr. and P.W.R.A., vol. 193, fo. 319.
[5] E. B. Pusey, *The Proposed Ecclesiastical Legislation*, 1874, pp. 6–7, 31, and 38.

Fig. 5

'Black Sheep' Archbishop Tait attempting to keep the ritualists in order by means of the Public Worship Regulation Bill.

complete disregard amongst the ritualists. Mackonochie refused Pusey's request to restrain the extremists, and his curate (Arthur Stanton) wrote that he cared 'none at all' for the Archbishop's bill, since he had been weaned long ago from the Established Church and learned to seek his nourishment elsewhere.[1]

More moderate High Churchmen still wished to kill the bill. As soon as Liddon read of it in *The Times* he consulted Salisbury and Sir Robert Phillimore in order to mount an attack. Phillimore consulted Gladstone. The President of the English Church Union sent a confidential letter to all members, 'as *Churchmen and not as members of the E.C.U.*', asking them to gather support for a deputation to Disraeli against the bill, led by Lord Marlborough. Dean Church inserted a notice in the newspapers inviting signatories for a similar public declaration. G. R. Mackarness, Bishop of Argyll and the Isles, claimed to have the support of 1,350 other clergymen in urging that the bill would be disastrous and that the ritual ought to be a matter for the minister's own discretion. As the debate became more heated, some of the extreme High Church party were reported to be drawing up a petition for the removal of archbishops and bishops from the House of Lords.[2]

Simultaneously the ritualists' opponents were using the same tactics. Magee contradicted Pusey 'by authority' in *The Times*, and Tory journals like the *Quarterly Review* urged that now was the ideal moment for legislation.[3] The 202 local branches of the Church Association were urged to make their influence felt, in opposition to the English Church Union.[4] In between these two bodies lay the Church Defence Association, a predominantly Tory body with the principal object of protecting the Church of England against disestablishment. Its members included, however, not only such fervent Protestants as the Father of the House of Commons, General G. C. W. Forester,

[1] Liddon, *Life of Pusey*, 1897, iv. 273 f. E. F. Russell, *A. H. Mackonochie*, 1890, pp. 220–6. G. W. E. Russell, *Arthur Stanton, a Memoir*, 1917, p. 148.

[2] J. O. Johnston, *Life and Letters of H. P. Liddon*, 1904, p. 178; J. G. Lockhart, *Charles Lindley Viscount Halifax*, 1935, i. 198; C. L. Wood's letter is bound up with A. J. Stephens and F. H. Jeune, *The P. W. R. Bill*, 1874, in Pusey House Library. M. C. Church, op. cit., pp. 241 f.; *Salisbury and Winchester Journal*, 25 July 1874, p. 3.

[3] MacDonnell, op. cit. ii. 4; Magee contradicted Pusey in other journals as well. *Quarterly Review*, July 1874, vol. 137, p. 246.

[4] *Eddows's Shrewsbury Journal*, 20 May 1874, p. 7.

and his nephew Cecil Forester, but also High Churchmen such as Lord Nelson and Beresford Hope. At a meeting on 8 May 1874, having received letters from both supporters and opponents of the Archbishop's bill, the Association decided to do nothing![1]

Parliament paid little attention to petitions got together in what it considered to be dubious ways. When two huge bundles, for and against, were carried into the Commons at the start of the second reading of the bill, they were greeted with 'cheers and laughter'.[2] However, these apparently monolithic blocks of signatures concealed the way in which the country, and indeed the petitioners, were divided over the bill. For instance, Lord Sandon (whose 'Orange fanaticism' Liddon considered even more heinous than the Lord Chancellor's)[3] presented a petition from the rural deanery of Prescott, apparently unanimously supporting the bill. In fact, three clergymen in that deanery had opposed it, one asserting that the Archbishop's remedy would prove worse than the disease.[4] A similar resolution from the ruri-decanal conference of Taunton expressed determined opposition to the ritualists. This was the attitude of the Vicar of Taunton, but only eighteen members of the conference supported him; seven voted against the petition, and several abstained. On the same day the powerful Principal of St. Aidan's College, Birkenhead, the Revd. Saumarez Smith, persuaded the ruri-decanal conference of the Wirral to send a message of support to the two archbishops. His proposal had been carried by only twenty-three votes to fourteen.[5]

Analysis of these petitions reveals that Pusey was wrong to assert that the laity favoured ritual even more than the clergy; but it is equally clear that, as the *Liverpool Mercury* concluded after the Wirral meeting, 'both clergy and laity in the deanery

[1] *Eddows's Shrewsbury Journal*, 18 Feb. 1874, p. 8, and 24 Oct. 1874, p. 2, for the Foresters' views. Also present at the C.D.A. meeting were Lord Harrowby, Sir John Kennaway, and the Bishop of Gloucester and Bristol.

[2] H. W. Lucy, *A Diary of Two Parliaments: The Disraeli Parliament, 1874–1880*, 2nd edn., 1885, p. 33.

[3] J. O. Johnston, op. cit., p. 178. For the opposition of Orangemen to ritualism see D. A. Roberts, 'The Orange Order in Ireland: a religious institution' in the *British Journal of Sociology*, vol. xxii, no. 3, Sept. 1971, pp. 269–82, esp. p. 276.

[4] *Liverpool Mercury*, 16 July 1874, p. 8, and the *Daily Courier*, 7 May 1874, p. 5.

[5] The *Parish Magazine of St. Mary Magdalene, Taunton*, June and July 1874. *Liverpool Mercury*, 16 June 1874, p. 6.

of Wirral are much divided in opinion, not only as regards
ritual but also on points of doctrine'. This division, the newspaper alleged, was by no means confined to the hundred of
Wirral.[1] The bill was now to face a similarly divided House of
Lords.

The Bill in the Lords

The debate in Parliament stirred deep passions. Tait rightly
described himself as being at the centre of a storm and although
he had tried to forearm himself by reading all the conflicting
articles and letters in the press, he suffered greatly from the
strain; at crucial moments in the debate he felt giddy and ill,
and was often thankful if he could get to bed by the small
hours of the morning.[2]

He introduced his proposals in a crowded House, the cor-
ridors filled with 'Deans and parsons, Broad, High, and Low,
as one might see at a glance by the cut of their cloth and the
trim of their beards'.[3] Tait foresaw that his chief problem
would lie with the High Church party, who indeed tripped
him up almost at once. He had drawn attention to such abuses
as censing, candles, acolytes, holy water, lenten ashes, models
of the Christ-child, and 'a figure or stuffed skin of a dove',
clearly implying that these were illegal Roman Catholic
practices imported into the Church of England by the ritualists.
He then went on to suggest that the ritualists were also using
altar cards at the eucharist, on which were prayers invoking
the Virgin Mary and the Apostles. Lord Nelson, however,
assured the House that on only three of these cards was the
name of the Virgin or of a saint to be found, and never in the
way of invocation. Tait (in an admission prudently omitted
by Randall Davidson in his account of the debate) was obliged
to confess that his statement might, 'perhaps, be regarded as
not strictly accurate if the word "invocation" is understood in
its technical and theological sense'. But he insisted that, though
he might be technically wrong, he was essentially right.[4]

---

[1] *Liverpool Mercury*, 16 June 1874, p. 6. The clergy vote was 12 for 10 against,
compared with the laity 11 for, 4 against; cf. the resolution lost at the Lincoln
Diocesan Conference in September 1874: 43 clergymen voted against the P.W.R.
Act, 54 for it. 7 laymen voted against it, 34 for.

[2] Tait Papers, Notebook 52, 26 Apr., 3, 14, and 17 May 1874.

[3] *Daily Courier*, 21 Apr. 1874, p. 5.   [4] Hansard, vol. 218, 788 f. and 1921 f.

Led by Lord Marlborough, the High Churchmen then moved that the bill be thrown out. Marlborough was important enough to have been offered the Lord-Lieutenancy of Ireland by Disraeli, and John Bright described him as an enlightened Conservative. His motion gained the approval not only of High Church peers like Bath, Beauchamp, Rutland, Nelson, and Limerick (who had tabled his own amendment to the bill), but also the unexpected support of the Bishop of Lincoln. But it was opposed in a long-winded speech by Lord Cairns, after which Lord Oranmore and Browne said his mind was so confused that it was only the fact that the High Church party seemed unanimously against the bill which made him still in favour of it. Limerick withdrew his amendment, but Marlborough's motion was crushingly defeated by 137 votes to 29. Ominously for Tait's plans, however, amongst those voting to throw out the bill were Lord Salisbury and the Bishop of Salisbury, while the Bishops of Lincoln and Oxford abstained.[1]

Because of Cairns's position in the Government, his intervention opposing Marlborough was important. He had also been intriguing behind the scenes with Lord Shaftesbury and Bishop Magee. Like Marlborough, Shaftesbury had intended to destroy the bill, but not for High Church reasons. He believed that ritualism 'and all its trumperies' were now matters of secondary consideration compared with the confessional, and because the bill made no attack on this 'foul thing', Shaftesbury had no time for it.[2] Moreover, Shaftesbury hated the bishops almost as much as he hated the ritualists. He believed that they had wrecked his own attempts to legislate against ritualism, and he had already been at work in the Lords to restrict their powers.[3] On the bill's second reading he proposed that a lay judge replace the bishop and his assessors, on the grounds that even if the bishops showed no partiality, to try ritual cases themselves would put them in a bad light: they were being asked to determine whether a prosecution should go forward at all, before being asked to pass into an adjoining room and try the whole issue again. He declared that even if he were sure of

---

[1] Hansard, vol. 219, 927, 938, 951. For Marlborough's stature see *The Diaries of John Bright*, ed. R. A. J. Walling, 1930, p. 514, and Monypenny and Buckle, *Life of Disraeli*, ii. 630.

[2] Quoted in Davidson and Benham, *Life of Tait*, ii. 197.

[3] Hodder, *Life of Shaftesbury*, pp. 618, 629, 635, 678.

Low Church bishops for the next half century, he would not confer on them the discretion contained in Tait's bill.[1] This was a popular Anglican attitude; Liddon was once surprised to find that the Liberal Warden Brodrick of Merton wanted to retain bishops in the Lords simply because he thought it kept them 'under the healthy influence of lay opinion'.[2] Shaftesbury now proposed to do the same for them in matters of ritual. His speech was torn to shreds by Magee, who pointed out his inconsistency in describing bishops as unfit to be judges when Shaftesbury's own bill in 1872 had proposed that each bishop be judge in his own diocesan court.

Magee sat down to cheers and the thanks of the archbishops, while Shaftesbury declared that he would have nothing more to do with the bill.[3] But Cairns played on his prejudice against bishops, and persuaded him to return at the committee stage of the bill on 4 June with proposals that in ritual cases a single lay judge, appointed by the archbishops, should represent the provinces of Canterbury and York, at a salary of £4,000 paid by the ecclesiastical commissioners. 'We shall make a good bill,' said Cairns, 'and the amendments, as coming from you, will have great weight.'[4] For Cairns, such amendments would have the additional advantage of not implicating the Government, and to this end Lord Salisbury was detailed to inform the House that the Cabinet neither supported nor opposed the bill. He added his own opinion that the bill would not deal with the abuses it was meant to correct, and he asked why the proposed lay judge was to be appointed by the archbishops; what was wrong with the usual custom of crown appointments?[5]

This behaviour by a senior member of the Government was embarrassing to the bill's supporters; but Tait believed that at least he knew where he stood with the rest of the Cabinet. He was, however, wrong: Disraeli and Cairns had no intention of revealing their plans.

[1] Hansard, vol. 219, 15–17.
[2] G. W. E. Russell, *Dr. Liddon*, 1905, p. 160; cf. the Earl of Shrewsbury during the debate: Hansard, vol. 219, 50.
[3] MacDonnell, *Life of Magee*, ii. 6; Hansard, vol. 219, 22 ff.; Hodder, op. cit., p. 682; cf. Shaftesbury's atack on the bill at the annual meeting of the Church Pastoral Aid Society, reported in the *Western Gazette*, 15 May 1874, p. 3.
[4] Hodder, op. cit., p. 683; Hansard, vol. 219, 950 f.
[5] Hansard, vol. 219, 955; cf. 50–5, for Salisbury's own views.

In order to keep the bishops in the dark, Cairns deliberately ignored a direct request for advice. Tait had written on 30 May, pointing out that he and Thomson would dine with the bishops the following Tuesday and that he would come to the Lords that day if Cairns wished to give him any information for them. He supposed, he wrote, that Cairns was 'not inclined' to Lord Shaftesbury's plan, 'and that the amendment really before us will be the Duke of Marlborough's'.[1] But Cairns waited until two days after the debate before he thought fit to tell the Archbishop of the secret arrangements with Shaftesbury.[2]

Archbishops Tait and Thomson, therefore, in ignorance of what was going on, both attacked Shaftesbury's proposals and then were obliged to change their minds in public when Cairns supported the proposals. Magee felt that it was 'something like treachery on the part of the government'[3] to go against what, as he understood, they had virtually agreed to previously. Thomson had just declared that the High Church clergy would never respect a secular court, while Tait had emphasized that they would respect a Church court;[4] however, both capitulated and voted for the lay judge. Shaftesbury's amendments were carried by 112 votes to 14. Their effect was to make certain that neither High Churchmen nor ritualists would find the Public Worship Regulation Act acceptable. Two bishops voted against them—Carlisle on the grounds that to put everything in the hands of a lay judge made the bishops no more than his humble servants, and Oxford because they gave a completely new penal character to the bill.[5]

Some of the High Churchmen, on the other hand, were delighted to hear Shaftesbury attack the bishops. Lord Bath now supported his amendments in the belief that they would do as little harm to the clergy as was compatible with such an objectionable bill. He only hoped that, for the protection of these clergy, Shaftesbury would be content to leave intact the bishops' power of veto over possible prosecutions.[6] Shaftesbury agreed, and went so far as to move the clause reintroducing this discretionary power. When the division came he acted

[1] Cairns Papers, P.R.O. 30/51/15. [2] Tait Papers, Notebook 52, 7 June 1874.
[3] MacDonnell, op. cit. ii. 8. [4] Hansard, vol. 219, 956–7.
[5] Ibid. 958. [6] Ibid.

as teller, but became so irritated at his own leniency that he voted against his own proposal![1] It was nevertheless carried.

Cairns now had no intention of letting the Lords alter any more of the bill. Since the beginning of May, Bishop Magee had been suggesting draft amendments to both Tait and the Lord Chancellor.[2] The latter—Cairns—determined to use these as 'a "red herring" across the scent', hoping that they would cause so much distraction that when they were withdrawn the remodelled bill would pass out of committee 'with universal consent, if not applause', and above all 'with the thankful approval of both Archbishops, most of the Bishops, Shaftesbury, Salisbury, Harrowby, Beauchamp and the Ritualists'. On 12 June Magee informed Tait that he had agreed to bring forward his amendments with the firm intention of withdrawing them when they had wasted enough time in the Lords.[3]

Three days later he proposed them in a crowded House. In a new clause to the bill he suggested seven points on which litigation should henceforth cease:

1. the use of the eastward position at the Eucharist;
2. the use of the words of administration at the Holy Communion other than separately to each communicant;
3. the use of hymns during divine services;
4. the celebration of Holy Communion at the time of Evening Service;
5. sermons at other services than Holy Communion;
6. the daily use of Morning and Evening Prayer;
7. the use of the Commination Service.

Magee said that his aim was merely to stop vindictive prosecutions, not to 'legalize any breach of rule, rubric, or canon'.[4] In fact there was no law against afternoon sermons, and Holy Communion had already been legally severed from Morning Prayer. Since real implication of his proposals was that Low Churchmen as well as ritualists might be failing to observe the

[1] Hansard, vol. 219, 1143–8.
[2] MacDonnell, op. cit. ii. 6; Cairns Papers, P.R.O. 30/51/15, 27 May 1874.
[3] Cairns to Disraeli, 12 June 1874, in Monypenny and Buckle, op. cit. ii. 663; Magee to Tait, 12 June 1874, in Tait Papers, Misc. Corr., vol. 193, fos. 186 ff.
[4] Hansard, vol. 219, 1569–72.

law, Cairns reinforced this by proposing that from now on the saying of the Athanasian Creed, which many Low Churchmen and all Broad Churchmen abhorred, should be optional (a proposition, said Magee, which would have had his strenuous opposition).[1] As the *Quarterly Review* commented, the Low Church party was being offered power to disuse the Commination Service in return for allowing the High Church party to use the eastward position.[2]

The Government's scheme worked. Since the amendments had been leaked some days before being proposed, they caused a furore before the debate in the Lords had even begun. Shaftesbury, who had been kept out of this part of the secret, told Cairns that if the amendments were carried they would 'sink the Bill in the Commons'. The Dean of Christ Church, Dr. Liddell, on the other hand, told Tait he found them entirely desirable.[3] When Magee dutifully withdrew them, he observed that he had received many letters, all differing about what should be excluded from litigation, and that many additions to his list had been proposed. His action provoked complaints. Lord Stanhope, for instance, said that the Bishop should have given earlier notice of his intended withdrawal, since he himself had planned to bring up the matter of the Athanasian Creed. (He had asked the Royal Commission on Ritual to make its use optional, but Bishop Wilberforce and the High Churchmen had defeated the proposal.[4]) But it was too late to object; after a few trivial squabbles, the committee stage of the bill was over.

Disraeli was beside himself with joy at the success of the conspiracy. He told Lady Bradford that he considered the affair to be 'one of the most successful, as it is certainly one of the most important, events in modern political history'. Bismarck, he believed, could not have done better; and the Church would be immensely strengthened, even if Lord Bath was furious and Lord Beauchamp resigned from the Cabinet.[5]

[1] Hansard, vol. 219, 1572; cf. Cairns, 938, on 4 June.
[2] *Quarterly Review*, vol. 137, p. 570.
[3] Cairns Papers, P.R.O. 30/51/8, 11 June 1874. Tait Papers, Misc. Corr., vol. 193, fos. 178 f., 6 June 1874. Pusey and Liddon expected the Archbishop's bill to include clauses minimizing Low Church 'heresies': Liddon, *Life of Pusey*, iv. 273.
[4] Hansard, vol. 219, 1571-2.   [5] Disraeli, *Letters*, i. 97-8.

Disraeli's manoeuvres meant that his government was still officially uncommitted to the bill;[1] they also ensured that the Archbishop had incurred the hostility of High Churchmen over a bill markedly different from the one he had intended to present. 'It is no longer the Archbishop's bill,' declared one ritualist after the second reading; 'it is Lord Shaftesbury's bill.'[2] In this form, after a perfunctory third reading, it reached the House of Commons.

The Bill in the Commons

The House of Commons consisted of 350 Conservatives, 245 Liberals, and 57 who supported Irish Home Rule. On 5 May, in the first important division of 1874, Disraeli's government had a majority of 61, and he guessed that on a critical occasion, given due notice, he could raise this to 80. In fact a week later he was delighted to find himself with a majority of 114.[3] Clearly, given government backing, the passage of the Public Worship Regulation Act was assured. Disraeli, however, still refused to declare himself.

This immediately caused difficulties for Tait, who was obliged to cast around for someone to introduce the bill in the Commons. Russell Gurney, the widely respected Recorder of London, refused, even though he told the Archbishop that he agreed with Lord Cairns's line on the matter. Lord Harrowby suggested Sir John Kennaway. After twelve days of anxiety, Tait received a letter from Kennaway saying that both he and Gurney were now prepared to offer themselves.[4] These negotiations did nothing to dispel Tait's fear that Disraeli would abandon him, and Dean Wellesley told him of a rumour that the Duke of Rutland was trying to persuade Bishop Magee to postpone all legislation on ritualism to the following year. The Bishop of Gloucester wrote urgently to express anxiety about the effect of Convocation on public opinion: 'Wait until the rubrics are settled and then legislate', was, he now feared, a very popular cry in certain quarters. On 8 July Tait told Disraeli that nothing

---

[1] As reiterated by the official government spokesmen, Richmond and Salisbury, Hansard, vol. 218, 808; vol. 219, 50.

[2] E. S. Grindle, *Canon or Statute*, 1875, p. 6.

[3] Disraeli, *Letters*, i. 84.

[4] Tait Papers, Misc. Corr., vol. 193: Gurney to Tait, 12 June, fo. 190; Harrowby to Tait, 10 June, fo. 198; Kennaway and Gurney to Tait, 22 June, fos. 204, 206.

which was said in Convocation should be taken to indicate that the bishops were wavering in their support for the bill. He pointed out that the Queen had asked him to press for early legislation: extended excitement of this kind was dangerous to the Church; to leave the bishops powerless for a year would lead to great evil.[1]

The first reading was on 26 June. On the afternoon of 9 July the bill was called for the second reading, in a House more crowded than at any time since the discussion of the sale of intoxicating liquors.[2] Gurney's introduction rehearsed the arguments that the bill 'would secure most thoroughly the fair rights of the clergy themselves', that they would soon come to consult their bishops as fathers and friends, that 'Englishmen would not recognise the law of the Church as opposed to the law of the land', and that the new act would make no new law or doctrine but simply concern itself with what was now unlawful.[3] The new Conservative member for Oxford, Mr. Hall, disagreed. The new court would not only have to administer law, but would also make it. He was ready to join with Mr. Knatchbull-Hugessen (at that time a faithful Gladstonian) in proposing that it was inexpedient to proceed with the bill. In support of this, Knatchbull-Hugessen asserted that many congregations, especially in towns, supported the innovations of the ritualist clergymen. For his part, he added, 'he protested against having either his doctrines or his symbols decided for him by a barrister of 10 years standing'.[4]

These were merely preliminary skirmishes before Gladstone himself rose to speak. On resigning office in 1874 he had also resigned the Liberal leadership, which was now divided between Lord Hartington in the Commons and Lord Granville in the Lords; but at his colleagues' request this had been kept secret, so that he still appeared to his opponents as 'Leader of that fantastic compound of sacerdotalism in religion and Radicalism in politics which had its birth in the Oxford Union'.[5] Achilles was returning to the fray, said the *Quarterly Review*, 'with the

[1] Tait Papers, Misc. Corr., vol. 193: Wellesley to Tait, 3 June, fos. 135 f.; Gloucester to Tait, fos. 218 f.; Tait to Disraeli (copy), fos. 226 ff.
[2] Lucy, *A Diary of Two Parliaments*, p. 33.
[3] Hansard, vol. 220, 1355–63.
[4] Ibid. 1365–70.
[5] F. Harrison in the *Fortnightly Review*, no. xv, Mar. 1874, p. 300.

THE AWAKING OF ACHILLES.

" MR. GLADSTONE declared that he had been constrained to quit his retirement to point out the false issue which had been laid before
Parliament, and to dispel the delusions and the ignorance which prevailed throughout the country in regard to the Bill."—*Morning Paper.*

FIG. 6

In the guise of Achilles, Mr. Gladstone re-enters politics to attack the
Public Worship Regulation Bill.

flame upon his head, and that voice, the very sound of which carried fear and confusion to the Trojan hearts'.[1] Gladstone's attack on the bill was violent. The bishops, he argued, were supporting a bill which no longer represented their original purpose and left them free to do whatever they pleased. He could produce eighteen examples where the law of the land was already being broken in churches; hymns during the offices, the neglect of the Athanasian Creed, and so on. All these would come under the new act, which would thus destroy the diversity in the Church of England that had developed not in the past ten or twenty years but since 1661. Gladstone's chief scorn was reserved for Clause 9, which secured the bishops' discretionary veto. 'Even if all the 27 Bishops of the present day are discreet, still there will come some fussy Bishop, or some Bishop who is fond of meddling, or who does not say "No" when to say "No" would be unpopular. . . . Through the little door opened by the one indiscreet or timid Bishop, there comes a judgment which overrides the discretion of the 26 wise Bishops and runs absolutely through the whole Kingdom.'[2]

He was insistent that the whole bill should be scrapped. In its place he laid six resolutions on the table, to be borne in mind if anyone wished to draw up a better bill at some time in the future. These urged that, first, the rubrics were out of date; secondly, it was wrong to restrict liberty in things indifferent; thirdly, the faults of individuals needed to be guarded against; fourthly, the House ought to be ready to draw up a bill against any design to alter 'the spirit or substance of the Established Religion'; fifthly, congregations should have rights; and sixthly, parliament and Church should jointly concur in matters of ecclesiastical law.[3]

Apart from their decided antagonism to the Archbishop's bill, these resolutions were so broad that even some of Gladstone's admirers found difficulty in giving them any precise meaning.[4] None the less, Liddon wrote to thank Gladstone for putting them forward. Most Conservatives, on the other hand, con-

[1] *Quarterly Review*, vol. 137, p. 572, quoting *Iliad* xviii. 203 ff.

[2] Hansard, vol. 220, 1382–3.

[3] Ibid. 1372 ff.

[4] *Letters on Church and Religion of W. E. Gladstone*, ed. D. C. Lathbury, 1910, i. 390 f.

demned them as 'a kind of general invitation to the House to
let the Ritualists alone to do as they like'.[1] They were, however,
supported from the Conservative front bench by the Secretary
for War, Gathorne-Hardy, whose speech met with such clam-
our from his fellow ministers that he had to appeal for a hearing.[2]
He argued that the bill would drive the moderates into the
ritualistic party. It would prosecute one parson for turning
east, and leave another alone for denying the divinity of Christ.
The House should listen to Convocation, which must be taken
as the voice of the clergy and the proper body to reform the
rubrics. For these reasons the bill ought to be deferred.[3]

Gathorne-Hardy's opinion was directly contrary to that of
Mr. Holt, a leading member of the Church Association; Holt
had already prepared a rival (and harsher) bill to put down
ritualists, but had written offering his support to Tait on 25
June.[4] In his view, he told the Commons, Convocation was quite
the wrong body to revise the two vital rubrics relating to the
ornaments of the clergy and the position of the minister at
the Eucharist. He deplored the fact that the Ritual Commission
had failed to remove the Catholic ambiguities in the rubrics.
And he produced a catena of quotations from ritualist sources
to remind the Commons of what they had to legislate against:
confession, reservation of the Sacrament, pre-Reformation
rituals, etc.[5]

The responses made by these men to the bill came as no
surprise to those who knew them. What no one expected was the
speech of Sir William Harcourt. Balfour's niece described
Harcourt as 'an Erastian undiluted', and Lord Halifax compared him to Titus Oates;[6] but, as former Solicitor-General
of the Gladstone administration, he was expected to try to
'pulverize' the Conservatives.[7] He had clearly gone to some
trouble over his speech, although one experienced observer
suggested that he must have astonished himself, let alone the

[1] C. Gladstone, *Mary Drew*, 1919, pp. 155–6; *Stockport Advertiser*, 24 July 1874,
p. 4.
[2] Lucy, op. cit., p. 34.
[3] Hansard, vol. 220, 1425–8.
[4] Tait Papers, Misc. Corr., vol. 193, fo. 216.
[5] Hansard, vol. 220, 1398.
[6] B. E. C. Dugdale, *A. J. Balfour*, 1936, i. 209; J. G. Lockhart, *Viscount Halifax*,
1936, ii. 126.
[7] T. H. S. Escott, *Platform, Press, Politics, and Play*, Bristol, n. d., p. 303.

House, by the amount of ecclesiastical knowledge he managed to bring to the subject after only a day or two of preparation.[1] What did astonish everyone was that his speech was not so much a criticism of the Conservatives as a personal attack on Mr. Gladstone.

The split in the Liberal leadership was now revealed for the first time since the election. Since the bill was not a governmental measure, said Harcourt, though he thought it should have been, the Opposition ought to have the same opportunity of disagreeing amongst themselves as the Tories had been allowed. He then turned on his former leader. 'They had all been under the word of the great enchanter tonight, and had listened with rapt attention as he poured forth the wealth of his incomparable eloquence.' But Gladstone's arguments contradicted Cranmer's decision, laid down in the preface to the Book of Common Prayer, that 'from henceforth all the whole realm shall have but one use'. A national church, as Harcourt understood it, 'was a Church founded upon the will of the Nation', and for this reason Parliament and the Crown had taken the Reformation out of the hands of Convocation. 'The Reformation was not established by the clergy but forced upon the clergy.' So today Parliament could deal with the rubrics, the catechism, hymn-singing, and the Athanasian Creed without the help of Convocation. Not surprisingly, Harcourt strongly objected to the bishops' veto, referring to it as a 'discretion . . . to determine whether the law should be enforced or not'. If, according to Gladstone, 4 per cent of the bishops were indiscreet, there must also be a considerable body of indiscreet lower clergymen. 'He knew of no remedy for that but forcing them to conform to the law.'[2]

It was a masterly and crushing speech, delighting the House[3] and including a cruel side-swipe at the unfortunate Mr. Hall whose delaying amendment had been praised by Gladstone. 'Owing, doubtless, to his inexperience as a member of that House,' said Harcourt, he had 'been so imprudent as to put down in his Resolution exactly what he meant.' In this he had deviated from the example of his leader![4] As a result of the

---

[1] J. McCarthy, *A History of Our Own Times*, 1879–80, iv. 415.

[2] Hansard, vol. 220, 1414–22.

[3] Escott, op. cit., p. 304.　　　　[4] Hansard, vol. 220, 1418.

speech, Conservative opinion speedily placed Harcourt 'in the very front rank of the parliamentary debaters of the age'.[1] Not all churchmen agreed. 'If I thought he was right', wrote the Bishop of Winchester, 'I would go in for disestablishment with all my heart.'[2] Gladstone was exceedingly angry, refusing to allow that any religious beliefs could have played a part in Harcourt's calculations. 'Even his slimy, filthy, loathsome eulogies upon Dizzy were aimed at me', he wrote. 'It is quite plain that he meant business, namely my political extinction.[3]

Pressure was now increasing to adjourn the debate. (Childers leapt up at one point to propose this while the speaker at that moment, J. G. Hubbard, was pausing merely for a glass of water.[4]) Before the adjournment was carried the Prime Minister was asked whether the Government would find any more time to debate the bill. With hindsight it was alleged that Disraeli 'saw that Mr. Gladstone was tampering with the sacred principles of the Reformation, and generously offered him a day for the development of his policy'.[5] In fact the Prime Minister was by no means so clear about what would happen, and was still cautiously feeling his way. On Childers's motion he said that, rather than find more time, he would prefer the debate to go on if possible. He deftly avoided responsibility by observing that 'this is a Bill of very great interest and importance, but it is to be deplored that it should have been sent down to the House of Commons so late in the session'.[6] When Forster, who was still confused by the Bishop of Peterborough's withdrawn resolutions,[7] urged an adjournment with a firm governmental promise of more time, Disraeli replied that he would give them his answer on the following Monday. Childers's motion was lost by 161 votes, and Colonel Pemberton immediately put the adjournment again, at which Disraeli said they should have no objection to going on till 4 a.m.: 'any unwillingness to do so was simply owing to the effeminate habits

---

[1] *Stockport Advertiser*, 14 Aug. 1874, p. 4.
[2] Tait Papers, Misc. Corr., vol. 193, 20 July 1874, fos. 230 f.
[3] Quoted in Magnus, *Gladstone, a Biography*, p. 197.
[4] Lucy, op. cit., p. 34.
[5] H. Paul, *A History of Modern England*, 1906, iii. 386.
[6] Hansard, vol. 220, 1438
[7] Tait Papers, Misc. Corr., vol. 193, Forster to Tait, 14 July, fo. 236.

which came over some people at this season of the year.'[1] This time the House rejected the adjournment by 243 votes. At this Colonel Makins moved the adjournment a third time. High Churchmen were now pressing for a longer debate. J. G. Talbot said he thought he was entitled to be heard on a subject which so vitally interested him. Lord Henry Scott said the Government had acted unfairly towards those members who still wished to speak, and Beresford Hope observed that two nights had been devoted to Home Rule and Scottish Patronage; surely the Church of England deserved more than one.[2] Disraeli acknowledged the will of the House; it might be possible, he said, to resume the debate on the following Wednesday. Harcourt still disagreed on the grounds that 'Wednesday would be a most undesirable day to proceed with a discussion, as a fluent orator like the honourable member for the University of Cambridge [Beresford Hope] might talk until 6 O'clock, and thus prevent the House from coming to a decision';[3] but a majority of 76 was now in favour of adjourning.

By agreeing to give more time to the bill, Disraeli threw overboard the Judicature and the Land Transfer Bills, which had already passed the Lords. Ritualists hoped by delaying the bill to prevent the House from coming to any decision at all. But in point of fact the adjournment to the following Wednesday was, as Shaftesbury confided to his diary, 'apparently a delay, really an advance',[4] since it was arranged that the debate would begin at noon and standing orders were to be suspended to allow it to go on, if necessary, for twelve hours. Liberals such as Walter Bagehot were sarcastic about the way in which Disraeli extended the debating time of the Commons. This was unfair, since during the previous ministry Gladstone had frequent recourse to special 'morning sittings' which lasted in fact from 2.00 p.m. to 7.00 p.m. on Tuesdays and Fridays (then normally private members' days).[5]

Disraeli's commitment was still, therefore, minimal, and the bill's supporters desperately continued to solicit him. The Dean of Windsor assured the Archbishop that 'Everything

[1] Hansard, vol. 220, 1440.   [2] Ibid. 1441–2.   [3] Ibid. 1442.
[4] Hodder, *Life of Shaftesbury*, p. 683.
[5] P. Fraser, 'The Growth of Ministerial Control in the 19th century House of Commons', *E.H.R.* lxxv, 1960, p. 456. W. Bagehot, *Collected Works*, ed. N. St. John-Stevas, 1968, iii. 493.

possible has been done here to urge d'Israeli to speak out.'[1]
In this uncertain situation, Convocation further distracted
Tait. On 12 July the clergy debated ritualism, and he noted
in his diary that 'Things looked very serious and I had to sum-
mon several of my suffragans from a distance, but by good
management all went well.'[2] The Queen was meanwhile
also trying to work on Mr. Gladstone, urging him through
Granville to stay away from the House on the excuse that his
brother-in-law had died on 17 June. Granville claimed to
have anticipated her request, but failed to persuade Gladstone
not to present his resolutions to the Commons. On 16 July he
wrote in confidence to the Queen that Gladstone might still
be persuaded to abandon them: 'Mr. Gladstone is not as
decided as he was on this point, and he may possibly give them
up, if he sees some amendment on which he can vote in
Committee.'[3]

Disraeli knew by now from his chief whip that very many
Conservative back-benchers supported the bill, and he was
under constant pressure from the Queen to proceed with it,[4]
but he refused to come out into the open without the full support of the Cabinet. By 11 July all except Salisbury were won
round; Disraeli said he was still unwilling to act unless they
were unanimous, whereupon Salisbury 'very unexpectedly . . .
said that he would not contend against the unanimous opinion
of his colleagues'. In reply to a cipher telegram from Victoria
urging the Prime Minister to show that he was 'in earnest
and determined to pass this Bill', he replied that he had 'passed
the Rubicon'. He was prepared for the resignation of some
colleagues, 'but the country is with your Majesty' and he
would see the matter through.[5]

On 14 July the Queen's hopes were realized. Two of Gladstone's closest lieutenants, Goschen and Forster, came out in
support of the bill.[6] Finally Disraeli spoke in its favour. Its
aim, he said, was 'to put down ritualism' and destroy 'the

[1] Tait Papers, Misc. Corr., vol. 193, Wellesley to Tait, 12 July, fo. 234.
[2] Tait Papers, Notebook 52, 12 July 1874.
[3] *Letters of Queen Victoria*, ii. 346.
[4] Hart Dyke to Disraeli, 10 July, Beaconsfield Papers, B/XII/F/61; Queen to
Disraeli, 10 July, Royal Archives D5/2, and 13 July; *Letters of Queen Victoria*, ii. 343.
[5] *Letters of Queen Victoria*, ii. 343.
[6] Hansard, vol. 221, 38–44 and 67–75.

Mass in masquerade'. His speech brought cheers from both
sides of the House.[1] Gladstone's aides brought him slips of
paper indicating next to no support for his resolutions,[2] and he
withdrew them without a division. As Shaftesbury put it, he
'slunk out of the House',[3] and the second reading was carried.
'*An immense triumph!*' boasted Disraeli to Lady Chesterfield;
'*Gladstone ran away.*'[4] Shaftesbury was filled with admiration
for the Prime Minister. 'Of all the clever men I know or have
ever known, D'Izzy is the chief. What a head he has for policy
and practice!'[5] The rejoicing was premature.

Dispute over the Veto

On 19 July Tait was certain the bill was won.[6] The committee
stage was expected to be a formality; several of the bishops
were planning not to return to the Lords merely to ratify what
had already been decided. But some observers noticed that the
Commons were in a dangerously Protestant mood. There was,
said Mundella, 'a most unpleasant tone of persecution in the
House'.[7] Even a moderate Evangelical like Canon Gray of
Liverpool believed that the bishops' veto was a flaw in the
legislation, since it might allow some erring ritualists to escape
prosecution; but he was prepared to accept it rather than risk
the bill.[8] Others felt more strongly about it. As the House went
into committee, Holt, speaking specifically on behalf of the
Church Association, proposed an amendment to allow an appeal
from the veto to the Archbishop. Russell Gurney accepted the
amendment; Gladstone led the High Churchmen in an attempt
to have it omitted, and was overwhelmingly defeated by the
Commons who approved the amendment by 103 votes to 37.[9]

The bill thus returned to the Lords on 3 August without the
veto. Archbishop Thomson had to upset an engagement with

[1] Hansard, vol. 221, 76–82; Lucy, op. cit., p. 35.
[2] *Quarterly Review*, vol. 137, p. 576.
[3] Hodder, op. cit., p. 683. Shaftesbury estimated that there were nearly 600 members present.
[4] Disraeli, *Letters*, i. 116.
[5] Diary, 18 July 1874, in Hodder, op. cit., p. 684.
[6] Tait Papers, Diary 19 July 1874, Notebook 52.
[7] Ibid., reported to Tait by W. C. Lake, 2 Aug. 1874; Misc. Corr., vol. 193, fo. 257; cf. *Annual Register, 1874*, 1875, p. 86.
[8] *Liverpool Mercury*, 30 June 1874, p. 6.
[9] Hansard, vol. 221, 888.

Baroness Burdett Coutts in order to return to the struggle, and he told Tait that the complications of the bill were now proving too much for him.[1] Tait was himself ready to give up the bishops' power of veto in order to retain the rest of the bill, and both archbishops decided to accept the Commons' amendment. Magee also agreed, but he prudently allowed his other appointments to keep him away from the Lords, although several bishops and peers had written urging his presence; it was clear, he said, that the removal of their absolute veto had put the other bishops in a 'great fluster', and that by voting with the archbishops he would be going against nearly all his brethren.[2] The Bishop of Bath and Wells declared that Holt's amendment threatened the bishop's 'natural and proper place as the friend of his Clergy'; he was none the less prepared to pay that price to keep the rest of the bill. The Bishop of Hereford disagreed; if he could get back to the House, he told Tait, he would now vote against the bill.[3] The Bishops of Oxford and Carlisle told Gladstone that they could not support the bill without the veto, and Gladstone himself charged the Bishop of Winchester to inform the archbishops that if the amended bill were accepted he held himself 'altogether discharged from maintaining any longer the Establishment of the Church'. Winchester agreed with his views,[4] and, with Rochester and Ely, refused to be swayed by the arguments of the archbishops on the morning of 3 August. Tait and Thomson went to the Bishops' room in the House of Lords, where they learned with alarm that seven of their suffragans would not vote for a bill containing Holt's amendment, and that Carlisle was determined to abstain.[5] Lincoln joined this meeting two minutes before the debate was to begin. Having been briefly informed of the views of Disraeli and Gladstone, he said that he too would oppose the amendment.[6]

[1] Tait Papers, Diary 2 Aug. 1874, Notebook 52.
[2] MacDonnell, *Life of Magee*, ii. 10.
[3] Tait Papers, Misc. Corr., vol. 193: A. C. Harvey to Tait, 2 Aug. 1874, fos. 255 ff.; Hereford to Tait, 3 Aug. 1874, fo. 261.
[4] Gladstone Papers, Additional MS. 44444, Oxford to Gladstone, 2 Aug. 1874; Carlisle to Gladstone, 12 Aug. 1874. Gladstone to Winchester in *Letters of Gladstone*, i. 393–4.
[5] Tait Papers, Diary 9 Aug. 1874, Notebook 52.
[6] Overton and Wordsworth, *Christopher Wordsworth*, pp. 259–60.

If the Lords deleted Holt's amendment, the bill was in jeopardy. Disraeli told the Archbishop that the Government and Gladstone were totally opposed to each other. He said that there were 200 men prepared to return to town at a moment's notice to throw out the whole bill if it were sent down from the Lords without the amendment.[1] Tait none the less went into the debate hopefully. Even though those bishops opposed to the amendment could count on the support of the High Church peers, the government chief whip in the Lords assured the Archbishop that 'Lord Salisbury and his crew' would be outvoted. Salisbury himself was pessimistic. 'The Protestant flood carries all before it,' he wrote in private to Gathorne-Hardy. 'I will see if anything can be done in the Lords—but I am not hopeful.' Even Gladstone believed that if the archbishops supported the amended bill, it would go through.[2]

He was wrong. Lord Salisbury urged the Lords not to give in to threats from the Commons, for these were mere 'bluster'.[3] Holt's amendment was rejected by 44 votes to 32. Lords Carnarvon and Carlton voted with Salisbury; and according to Disraeli four lords-in-waiting followed them into opposition by error![4] The Lords also threw out the Commons' amendment designed to stiffen the bill by bringing within the scope of its provisions collegiate churches and cathedrals. The Commons, Tait said, were 'determined that St. Paul's would not be made a Mass House'; but in this matter, as well as over the veto, he was forced to admit that the High Church bishops were 'looking out to defend their own rights against the Archbishops'.[5]

'Things are as bad as possible,' wrote Disraeli. 'I think the Bill is lost.'[6] Tait went to bed convinced that six months' work had been wasted: Harcourt, Gurney, Kennaway, and Holt had all called on him to say that they and the Lords were irreconcilable. But by the next morning the Archbishop was

---

[1] Tait Papers, Misc. Corr., vol. 193, Disraeli to Tait, 3 Aug. 1874, fos. 262 ff.

[2] Tait to Wellesley: returned letter bound with Tait's Diary, 7 Aug. 1874, Notebook 52. Salisbury to Gathorne-Hardy, 29 July 1874, in Salisbury Papers, D/29/11. Gladstone, *Letters*, i. 393.

[3] Hansard, vol. 221, 1253.

[4] Disraeli, *Letters*, i. 122.

[5] Tait to Wellesley, in letter of 7 Aug. 1874, loc. cit.

[6] Disraeli, *Letters*, i. 121.

determined to reconcile them, and he discovered that after a night's sleep and under the influence of a conciliatory article in *The Times*, Gurney and Kennaway had changed their minds. He received a note from the Duke of Richmond which said that almost everything depended on the line taken by Harcourt, and Tait tracked the latter to his club, 'got him into my carriage, and urged wiser counsels'. He then tried to persuade Holt to abandon his amendment.[1] Shaftesbury too was negotiating with members of Parliament, having put off his plans to leave for Chillingham at Cairns's request. But he found that Salisbury's intemperate language about the Commons had offended many.[2]

At noon on 5 August the debate began. Gurney urged the Commons to accept their defeat in the Lords. Harcourt agreed, and then proceeded to vilify the Lords, Gladstone, and Salisbury for one and a half hours. Gladstone called it 'a frantic tirade, extremely bad in tone and taste, and chiefly aimed at poor me'. With the veto restored, however, he said that he and High Churchmen had no more objections to the bill.[3]

He was extremely glad to withdraw. As his previous anger at Harcourt had revealed, Gladstone knew that in defending the ritualists he was taking up a dangerously vulnerable political position. He had received warnings that some of his supporters were finding it hard to go along with him. In the heat of the battle, J. G. Talbot, for example, had told Mrs. Gladstone that he urgently needed to discuss the whole affair with her husband, adding, 'I wish we were all out of this uncomfortable business: but we must try to keep cool.'[4] Gladstone knew that he was presenting himself in a false light in many respects. He was not even a ritualist himself. They had given great offence, he explained to Dr. Döllinger, but he defended them because they also perhaps 'had a considerable influence on stopping the secessions, which were a greater and more serious mischief than any that indiscretion on their part can bring'.[5] As he told

---

[1] Tait Papers, Diary 9 Aug. 1874, Notebook 52, and letter to Wellesley of 7 Aug. 1874, loc. cit.

[2] Diary 5 Aug. 1874, in Hodder, *Life of Shaftesbury*, p. 684.

[3] Gladstone, *Letters*, i. 395.

[4] Gladstone Papers, Additional MS. 44444, letter from J. G. Talbot, 15 July 1874.

[5] Ibid., Additional MS. 44140, letter to Döllinger, 21 Apr. 1874.

Harrowby in private, he wanted the militants on both sides to come together and find a *modus vivendi*, so as not to precipitate disestablishment.[1]

The state of his mind is revealed by the private memorandum about his political future, which he composed with many alterations and deletions at the beginning of 1875. The final anxious conclusion merits reading in full:

The course which I felt it my duty to take last Session with regard to the Public Worship Bill, egregiously (and in some cases even wantonly) misunderstood as I may think it to have been, unquestionably gave offence to some members of the Liberal party, and rendered it doubtful policy for me to rely upon the ties which have heretofore bound us together, until we shall have learned what is likely to be the further course of this Government and of Parliament with respect to questions of this dangerous class.[2]

Such an assessment must have been immensely painful to one who never ceased to believe that 'a political position is mainly valuable as instrumental for the good of the church', under which rule every other question became 'one of detail only'.[3]

Disraeli too was under some political stress. In the Commons he could not refrain from insulting Salisbury, describing him as 'a great master of gibes and flouts and jeers'; but the Prime Minister now accepted the Lords' decisions.[4] Only the Evangelical Newdegate (who in 1871 had proposed a bill for the suppression of monasteries and nunneries) walked out to show his disapproval.[5] At two o'clock Tait wrote to the Queen from the Lords: 'Thank God, the bill has passed.' A letter from Disraeli told her that it had passed without a division. It was his second letter to her that day; he had written in the morning to say the bill was in extreme danger.[6]

Protestants rejoiced. Archdeacon Denison's churchwarden

---

[1] Gladstone Papers, Additional MS. 44444, letter to Harrowby, 10 Oct. 1874.

[2] Ibid., Additional MS. 44762, fo. 150. Headed 'Private No. 2', from Hawarden, Jan. 1875.

[3] *The Gladstone Diaries, Vol. III, 1840–1847*, ed. M. R. D. Foot and H. C. G. Matthew, 1974, p. 53, 16 Aug. 1840; and in J. Morley, *Life of Gladstone*, 1903, i. 182. On the centrality of Gladstone's religion in his life see the comments of the editor, pp. xxxi f., in *The Gladstone Diaries, Vol. I, 1825–1832*, ed. M. R. D. Foot, 1968.

[4] Hansard, vol. 221, 1359.

[5] *Stockport Advertiser*, 14 Aug. 1874, p. 4.

[6] Tait Papers, Diary 9 Aug. 1874, Notebook 52; *Letters of Queen Victoria*, ii. 351.

would have rung the church bells had he not discovered Denison himself sitting in the tower, armed with 'formidable and dangerous weapons'.[1] Gladstone's circle took comfort from the thought that his success over the veto was a 'triumph', in view of his 'small and disorganised party'. 'All is peace and harmony', wrote Shaftesbury. In fact, the support given to Gladstone by Carnarvon and Gathorne-Hardy, along with Disraeli's rebuke to Salisbury, had created considerable speculation that the three Conservative rebels would have to resign.[2] Salisbury was by far the most important; both he and Disraeli realized that they had gone too far, and they immediately set about making peace. On the evening of the debate Disraeli wrote that his real intention had been to defend Salisbury against the attacks of Harcourt: 'I conceived a playful reply to his invective, but what was not perhaps ill-conceived was, I fear, ill-executed.' Salisbury replied that he was 'too much accustomed to speak my own mind with very little restraint, to complain if others in the course of their argument find it necessary to fall foul of me.'[3]

At this point a breach which had lasted over eight years began to be healed, and in 1876 Salisbury refused Lord Bath's invitation to him to join the campaign against Disraeli's handling of the Bulgarian Atrocities, explaining that 'Since the Public Worship Regulation Bill we have worked together without friction.' Lord Bath fully expected the co-operation of Salisbury, who ten years previously had told him that 'so long as Disraeli is leader of the party in the Commons, we in the Lords must follow the course that seems wisest without much reference to the action that may have been taken by Conservatives in the other House.'[4] Salisbury followed that policy for the last time during the debate over the Public Worship Regulation Bill.

[1] The *Western Gazette*, 21 Aug. 1874, p. 6, and H. P. Denison, *Seventy-Two Years*, p. 59.

[2] *The Diary of Lady Frederick Cavendish*, ed. J. Bailey, 1927, ii. 173; Hodder, op. cit., p. 684; *Liverpool Mercury*, 7 Aug. 1874, p. 6.

[3] Salisbury Papers, D/20/47 and 49; and in Lady G. Cecil, *Life of Robert Marquis of Salisbury*, iii. 61.

[4] Salisbury to Bath, 8 Feb. 1876 and 5 Nov. 1866, in Bath Papers, Longleat, Muniments E. This evidence contradicts the statement in Monypenny and Buckle, *Life of Disraeli*, ii. 624 f., that Salisbury and Disraeli were reconciled at the beginning of 1874.

On 7 August the Queen saw Disraeli at Osborne. 'She was wreathed with smiles, and, as she talked, glided about the room like a bird.' She told him that the bill had been passed entirely as a result of his courage and tact. 'To think of your having the gout all the time,' she said; 'How you must have suffered!' And she made him take a chair. To Tait, the Queen wrote that to have lost the bill would have constituted a triumph for the ritualists, who had done so much 'to poison the minds of the younger and higher classes'. She told the Dean of Windsor that if her 'faithful Commons' had rejected the bill, she would have abdicated in favour of the Stuarts.[1]

Votes and Explanations

At some point in the debate almost every important figure, lay or clerical, had been forced into a volte-face; but there was of course an underlying consistency in the way they were reacting to the various stages of the bill. By far the strongest consideration in both Houses of Parliament was the notion that the ritualists were romanizers. 'The only belief much felt', said W. E. Forster, 'is that we are not and will not be papists.'[2] According to John Walter, M.P. for Berkshire and chief proprietor of The Times, 'Popery' was 'not a fit religion for Englishmen'. He had once supported the Tractarians, but now he told the Commons that the changes in vestments and ritual since Newman's Anglican days had been made with the 'precise and deliberate intention' of driving men to Rome. Ritualism, Lord Teignmouth asserted, was 'Ultramontanism' under a pretence of religion.[3] These men therefore voted for the bill. Many others supported it because they still conceived of Roman Catholicism as a threat to English liberties. In imitating Catholics, said Cecil Forester, M.P. for Wenlock, the ritualists stood for both 'the doctrine of the mass and the tyranny of the priesthood'. After the debate Lord Portsmouth declared himself more than ever convinced that 'the State was the bulwark of Protestantism, of free thought, and of religious

---

[1] Disraeli, Letters, i. 129; Letters of Queen Victoria, ii. 351; Wellesley quoted in Tait's Diary, 19 July 1874, Notebook 52.

[2] To Tait, 14 June 1874, Tait Papers, Misc. Corr., vol. 193, fo. 237.

[3] S. Morison, History of The Times, 1939, ii. 46; Salisbury and Winchester Journal, 28 Nov. 1874, p. 2.

liberty', since a clergy free from State interference meant simply priestcraft, which he abhorred.[1] In voting to put down the ritualists such men believed they were striking a blow for freedom.

Other Protestants could scarcely conceal their disappointment that the provisions of the bill were not harsher. Holt's bill, they felt, would have been 'a step in the right direction'.[2] The religion of these men was completely Erastian; ritualist pretensions only confirmed in them a distrust of all clergymen. In 1873 Holt had asked for Magee's help in stopping confession, and Magee had replied that those who were loudest in demanding that bishops suppress erroneous doctrines were also 'the most jealous of the slightest addition to those very limited powers which bishops now possess'.[3] Holt's behaviour during the debate of 1874 proved Magee right. This Erastian dislike of what Harcourt called 'the new claims of the Anglican priesthood' was shared by the Whigs. On their behalf the *Edinburgh Review* welcomed the Public Worship Regulation Act as 'a confirmation of our convictions'.[4] In 1874 such men took comfort in the thought that Church of England clergymen were 'as much under contract to conform to certain regulations as civil service clerks'.[5]

To this pattern of English Protestantism, the Orange convictions of men like Lord Cairns and Lord Sandon brought prejudices arising from centuries of hatred and economic discrimination between Catholics and Protestants in Ireland. In Britain, Orange beliefs were strongest in Liverpool and Scotland, which contained areas of high Irish immigration. Liverpudlians believed in 1874 that the spirit of the Prince of Orange could alone once again save them from the threatened tyranny of Rome.[6] (When the West Derby Board of Guardians investigated complaints of ritualism in the workhouse chapel, it was said that the chaplain was an Orangeman and therefore 'above suspicion'.[7]) On his visit to Scotland in 1874, Disraeli

---

[1] *Eddows's Shrewsbury Journal*, 24 Oct. 1874, p. 2; 28 Oct. 1874, p. 7.

[2] *Stockport Advertiser*, 24 Apr. 1874, p. 4.

[3] MacDonnell, *Life of Magee*, i. 293.

[4] Harcourt reported in *Salisbury and Winchester Journal*, 26 Dec. 1874, p. 3; *Edinburgh Review*, Oct. 1974, p. 428.

[5] *Northern Echo*, 22 Apr. 1874, p. 3.   [6] *Daily Courier*, 19 May 1874, p. 6.

[7] *Staffordshire Sentinel*, 17 Oct. 1874, p. 4.

acknowledged the importance of the Orange Order in his political calculations. The provincial grand lodge of the North Eastern District described him as the only person able to save the country from ritualists and Roman Catholics, and the Prime Minister professed himself 'greatly honoured by this'.[1] The views of these Orangemen contrasted sharply with those of the supporters of Irish Home Rule, who were either themselves Roman Catholics or had come to terms with Catholicism in Ireland. Twelve Home Rule supporters voted against the Public Worship Regulation Bill, and all but one of the rest abstained.

The Protestants in Parliament far outnumbered the Anglo-Catholics. High Church convictions spread in families, and Gladstone's attacks on the bill were supported by various relatives (W. H. Gladstone, Lord Lyttelton, Lord Frederick Cavendish, John Gilbert Talbot) as well as by some faithful followers who were not ritualists, for instance, John Emerich Dalberg-Acton, Sir Mountstuart Grant Duff, Edward Hugessen Knatchbull-Hugessen, William Rathbone, and Sir Arthur Wellesley Peel. Independent Liberals, such as Robert Lowe, Edward Horsman, and Samuel Laing also supported Gladstone's opposition, and the group was enlarged through the influence of Salisbury. His nephew, Arthur James Balfour, had entered Parliament as Salisbury's protégé in 1874, and although he was no High Churchman he too voted against the bill. Salisbury's friend since school-days, Lord Carnarvon, was a more important ally against Disraeli. Another Conservative supporter was William Heathcote, whom Salisbury described in 1874 as 'the only man in England whose political judgment in party questions I much respect—and who hates Disraeli as much as I do'.[2] Salisbury could also count on the support of Lord Bath's family connections, who included the M.P. for South Wiltshire (Lord Henry Thynne), Viscount de Vesci, and Lord de la Warr. Other Tory aristocrats opposing the bill were Lord Henry Gordon-Lennox, the Earl of Devon, a daughter of whom was married to the president of the E.C.U., and Lord Nelson, who had been converted to ritualism at Trinity College, Cambridge.

In view of Trinity's role in the development of ritualism, it is

[1] *Dundee Advertiser*, 13 Oct. 1874, p. 2.   [2] Cecil, *Life of Salisbury*, ii. 44.

not surprising that a number of Members of Parliament who had been educated there opposed the bill. They included Hugh Culling Eardley Childers, Lord Frederick Cavendish, Sir William Stirling Maxwell, Edward Horsman, Lord John Manners, Alexander James Beresford-Hope, and Henry Cecil Raikes. Raikes was chairman of the executive committee of the Church Defence Institution, which (unlike the Church Defence Association) had no objection to using the word 'catholic' of the Church of England.[1] Another prominent member of the C.D.I., the Conservative M.P. for Mid-Cheshire Wilbraham Egerton, voted against the bill because he felt that the Church of England should be 'comprehensive both in its doctrine and ritual'. He believed that only bona fide churchmen, rather than a 'Parliament prejudiced against a small section of the clergy', should legislate in church matters.[2] Algernon Egerton, Conservative M.P. for South-east Lancashire, joined him in opposition to the bill.

No member of the C.D.I. wanted disestablishment. Algernon Egerton said that the union between Church and State was 'more necessary for the State than for the Church.'[3] But a far more radical group agreed with the view that Parliament was no longer a suitable body to legislate for the Church. At its November meeting, the Liberation Society adopted almost unanimously a motion that the passing of the Public Worship Regulation Act supplied a striking illustration of the danger of state interference in religious matters.[4] Henry Richard (president of the Liberation Society in 1874), Edward Jenkins, P. A. Taylor, Ll. Dillwyn, R. M. Carter, and A. J. Mundella all agreed with Jenkins that 'Establishments were inequitable and inexpedient as a matter of politics, and as a matter of religion injurious to the purest Christianity',[5] and consequently voted against the bill. 'We shall be much more religiously happy', said the Anglican radical M.P. for Bolton, J. K. Cross, 'when all such like things are beyond the domain of Parliamentary control.'[6]

---

[1] *Eddows's Shrewsbury Journal*, 9 Sept. 1874, p. 7.

[2] W. Egerton, *Revision of the Rubrics*, 1874, p. 15; J. C. Williams, *The Demand for Freedom in the Church of England*, 1883, p. 15 and n.

[3] *Eccles and Patricroft Journal*, 28 Nov. 1874, p. 5.

[4] *Dundee Advertiser*, 6 Nov. 1874, p. 7.

[5] Ibid., 11 Dec. 1874, p. 6.

[6] *Bolton Evening News*, 6 Jan. 1875, p. 4.

Henry Fawcett reminded his Brighton constituents of 'the folly that my be committed by Parliament when it gives way to Protestant panic', and said he refused to fetter the Church in the bonds of a narrow conformity.[1] Lord Randolph Churchill[2] and Fawcett's radical friend Lord Fitzmaurice agreed, and all three voted against the bill.

Such views were summed up by Campbell-Bannerman, the future Prime Minister, in an address to his Stirling constituents at the end of the year. Although he was no ritualist, Campbell-Bannerman strongly believed in individual liberty; opinions could not be put down by legislation. In any case, he said, the bill had been badly thought out and Disraeli had waited 'till he saw what way the cat was going to jump'. The Prime Minister had forgotten that the Church of England was comprehensive, resting 'one side on Rome and another on Geneva'. Finally, it was ridiculous for a parliament that included Roman Catholics, Nonconformists, Unitarians, 'Jews, Turks, infidels and heretics', to legislate for the Anglican Church.[3]

But however cogently the opponents of the bill might argue, they had no chance of stopping it. Far too many members of the Lords and Commons in 1874 agreed with Lord Hampton's opinion that one might tolerate Roman Catholics but never Anglican ritualists. As he told the Worcester Church Defence Association at the end of August, the passing of the bill proved that 'neither the Liberation Society nor the Ritualistic clergy' could 'impair the integrity and efficiency of the Church'.[4]

[1] *Salisbury and Winchester Journal*, 22 Aug. 1874, p. 2.
[2] J. W. Derry, *The Radical Tradition*, 1967, p. 281. The religious convictions of Lord Randolph and the Churchills are analysed in R. E. Quinault, 'The Fourth Party and the Religious Opposition to Bradlaugh', *E.H.R.*, vol. xci, no. 359, Apr. 1976, pp. 320–2.
[3] *Dundee Advertiser*, 20 Nov. 1874, p. 7.
[4] *Eddows's Shrewsbury Journal*, 26 Aug. 1874, pp. 5 and 7.

IV

THE CONSEQUENCES

Intransigence

S OME hoped that the act would never be used. Mr. Heath, a
new Conservative M.P. in 1874, had voted for it as a stand
for Protestantism, but he said that he hoped the bishops
and clergy would sort out almost every dispute without reference
to it. A deacon in Dorset felt that the original bill had been so
much altered that no bishop could possibly prosecute under it.[1]

Some of the bishops were clearly distressed by what had
happened. The insolence of the Erastians had shocked them,
and their own public image, they had been told, was not
what they imagined.[2] At the same time Tait's attempts to
override them had created 'a very rebellious team', according
to Magee.[3] Oxford, Lincoln, and Salisbury had made it plain
in the Lords that they now totally opposed the bill. Selwyn of
Lichfield had taken no part in the debate, telling his Diocesan
Conference that he 'shrank from' the notion of enforcing the
law against deviant clergymen. Even though Harvey Goodwin
of Carlisle believed that something was needed to curb excess,
he had travelled to London purposely to oppose any appeal
from the bishop's veto; now he told his diocese that he hoped
the act would be invoked as little as possible. It was something
like an ironclad ship or a monster gun—a warning rather than
a weapon of offence.[4]

These, however, were not typical views. Ellicott accused
those who urged moderation of seeking popularity. Winchester,
he wrote, was currying favour with the Lower House of Convocation because he did not like 'Lincoln being the Hero of

---

[1] R. Heath in *Staffordshire Sentinel*, 17 Oct. 1874, p. 7; an unnamed deacon in
Salisbury and Winchester Journal, 11 July 1874, p. 6.

[2] Winchester to Tait on the Erastians, 13 Aug. 1874, Tait Papers, Misc. Corr.,
vol. 193, fo. 292; Leatham in Hansard, vol. 220, 1434.

[3] MacDonnell, *Life of Magee*, ii. 12.

[4] Selwyn in *Eddows's Shrewsbury Journal*, 10 June 1874, p. 6; H. Goodwin in
Liverpool Mercury, 28 Aug. 1874, p. 7.

the High Church'. Ellicott had publicly expressed his opinion that the bill was inadequate, because, as he later explained to Tait, he really wanted to goad the ritualists into secession.[1] However, he was ready to use it *faute de mieux*, as were the rest of the bishops with varying degrees of enthusiasm. On 8 March 1875 they attempted to disguise their differences by publishing an equivocating declaration of intentions in *The Times*. Selwyn signed it because he thought it showed moderation over the eastward position. Salisbury and Baring of Durham refused to sign. Baring publicly stated that the declaration was insufficiently hostile to the ritualists. Archbishop Thomson had not had the courage to follow his example, although he wished to do so.[2]

If bishops were prepared to allow prosecutions, Bishop Jackson's prophecy that the act would bring peace and serenity to the Church[3] could only come to pass if the ritualists now voluntarily gave up their irritating practices. Ellicott believed that they would in fact try to make a deal with the bishops, and he was determined to resist such an attempt in his diocese.[4] But none was made anywhere: the ritualists had already developed a tradition of resistance to the law, and they drew upon it now. In 1871, after the Purchas judgement had condemned ritual, the Revd. A. D. Wagner had circulated the bishops with a pamphlet explaining why such judgements would be disobeyed. He sent round a second edition in 1874. Ritualists advised each other to settle their goods on their wives and children, as the Revd. John Purchas had done.[5] Archdeacon Denison said that now, as before, he was ready to be deprived rather than give up ritual. A Staffordshire vicar wrote to Lord Selborne that the 'only chance of bad law giving way to good law is for it to be disobeyed'.[6] In November the E.C.U. passed

[1] Ellicott to Tait, 10 Aug. 1874 and 10 Feb. 1875, in Tait Papers, Misc. Corr., vol. 193, fos. 282 f. and vol. 210, fo. 139. See the report in the *Western Gazette*, 15 May 1874, p. 13, for his dislike of the bill.
[2] Thomson to Tait, 16 Feb. 1875, Tait Papers, Misc. Corr., vol. 210, fo. 185; Selwyn to Tait, 12 Feb. 1875, ibid., fo. 142; Baring in *The Times*, 11 Mar. 1875.
[3] J. Jackson, *Our Present Difficulties*, 1875, pp. 64–5.
[4] Ellicott to Tait, 10 Aug. 1874, Tait Papers, Misc. Corr., vol. 193, fo. 283.
[5] A. D. Wagner, *Reasons for Disobeying on Principle*, 1874. H. W. Holden, *The Coming Campaign: How it will be won*, 1874, p. 3.
[6] G. A. Denison, *A Charge of the Archdeacon of Taunton at his Visitation*, 1874, p. 8. *A Letter on the Present State of Confusion in the Church of England*, by a Country Vicar, Rugeley, 1874, p. 6.

a resolution not to recognize the new court and to take legal advice as to the best means of resistance.[1]

The act provided that appeals from the new lay judge should be to the Judicial Committee of the Privy Council. The ritualists' opposition to this was part of their Tractarian inheritance. As Newman said, the Tractarian movement started 'on the ground of maintaining ecclesiastical authority as opposed to the Erastianism of the State'.[2] The Judicial Committee of the Privy Council had replaced Henry VIII's High Court of Delegates as a result of the legislation of 1833; but no one had envisaged that it would eventually deal with issues of doctrine or ritual. Mackarness described it as 'an anomalous tribunal, notoriously constituted for a totally different purpose'.[3] High Churchmen had hated it since the Gorham judgement. Now Wagner told his bishop that if he were brought before such a body he would neither recognize nor submit to it. The Privy Council, said the Revd. J. Bell Cox, was a purely secular body whose judgements 'in spiritual matters have no force'. Fortified by these beliefs, the ritualists determined to destroy the act 'without striking a blow . . . by patient, passive resistance'.[4]

Their campaign to discredit it was unexpectedly helped by the man appointed as its first judge. Lord Selborne turned the job down. The Home Secretary, Richard Cross, had put forward the name of James Plaisted, Baron Penzance. Although Penzance was known to be a Liberal in politics, Disraeli declared himself 'quite satisfied'.[5] The ritualists were not. In their opinion he was 'neither known to be "learned" nor at all "practised in ecclesiastical laws" '. He possessed, said Bell Cox, 'no spiritual authority whatever'.[6] Worst of all, he had made his name in the Divorce Court.

Penzance was in fact both civilized as a person and com-

---

[1] The *Western Gazette*, 6 Nov. 1874, p. 2.

[2] J. H. Newman, *Difficulties of Anglicans*, 1850, p. 114.

[3] Mackarness, *A Charge delivered to the Diocese of Oxford*, p. 22.

[4] A. D. Wagner, *Christ and Caesar, Part II: a Letter to the Lord Bishop of Chichester*, 1877. J. B. Cox, *Correspondence between the . . . Bishop of Liverpool and the Revd. J. Bell Cox*, Liverpool, 1880, p. 6. Holden, op. cit., p. 3.

[5] Cross Papers, British Library, Additional MS. 51265, Disraeli to Cross, 30 July 1874. Cf. R. Palmer, *Memorials, Part II: Personal and Political, 1865–1895*, 1898, i. 353 f.

[6] A. H. Mackonochie to the Royal Commission on Ecclesiastical Courts, *Report*, 1883, p. 286. J. Bell Cox, op. cit., p. 5. Cf. Denison, *Notes of My Life*, p. 63.

petent as a lawyer. *Vanity Fair* had described him as 'the Judge of dissolution', adding that he gave to the entanglements of his work 'an impartial attention, calculated to satisfy all but the defeated parties to the dispute'.[1] He was tall and dignified, and more than anything else he loved roses. (Compelled to work in London, he bought land at Clapham in order to grow them, but the increasing fog and smoke of the metropolis killed off his favourite flowers.) In 1872 he had retired from the Divorce Court because of ill health; but he soon recovered, and did not die until 1899 at the age of eighty-three. His declining years were devoted to a judicial summing up of the Bacon–Shakespeare controversy, which unfortunately gave him a reputation for eccentricity.[2]

Whatever Penzance's personal qualities, it was a tactical error to authorize a man experienced in divorce proceedings to sit in judgement on the clergy. But any appointment would have irked the ritualists, because it showed that the new act was to have teeth. As one of Gladstone's High Church correspondents wrote, 'If the new judge is to be wholly occupied with cases, that implies permanent litigation.' It also took away the High Churchmen's confidence that Convocation would protect their interests when it came to revising the rubrics in the Book of Common Prayer. 'To appoint a new judge to deal with Laws which Convocation is now authorized to review, is like assuming that Convocation will make *ambiguous* Rubrics or Regulations, or will leave the existing (*alleged*) ambiguous Rubrics in their present condition.'[3]

The archbishops themselves were soon embarrassed by the appointment of Penzance. There had been a squabble in the Commons about the new judge's salary, and Gladstone had managed to prevent the money from being paid by the Ecclesiastical Commission. Disraeli did not dare press a scheme to pay it out of state resources and said that the judge (as yet unnamed) would be satisfied with his existing pension. Pen-

---

[1] *Vanity Fair*, 18 Dec. 1869: Judges No. 2, Lord Penzance (where Penzance is also identified as a Liberal).

[2] J. P. Wilde, Baron Penzance, *The Bacon–Shakespeare Controversy: a judicial summing-up*, ed. M. H. Kinnear, 1902. The biographical information is derived from pp. vi–viii of a note contributed to this work by F. A. Inderwick.

[3] Gladstone Papers, Additional MS. 44444, letter from the Vicar of Ardleigh, 8 July 1874.

zance, however, said he wished to be paid, so the archbishops told Disraeli that they would work out a scheme themselves.[1] They failed to pay Penzance properly till 1877 when the Registrar of the Faculties Court died, and Tait (on his own authority) handed over most of the faculty fees. Penzance further upset the archbishops (and horrified High Churchmen)[2] by declaring that his appointment was a statutory one, which did not require him to take canonical oaths, subscribe to the Thirty-nine Articles, or accept any ecclesiastical mandates.[3] These had formerly been part of the formalities for appointing a new Dean of Arches. When the idea of a lay judge had been sprung on the archbishops during the debate in the Lords, Thomson had tried to maximize the judge's ecclesiastical authority by suggesting that he assume the offices of Dean of Arches, principal of the Chancery Court of York, and Master of the Faculties, as soon as these fell vacant. In the event, when Sir Robert Phillimore resigned as Dean of Arches in 1875, the Queen's Bench decided that Penzance should not have it, in spite of the Lords' decision.[4] The Lord Chief Justice said that Penzance's court was an entirely new creation, not intrinsically related to the old Court of Arches.[5] A humiliating consequence of this decision was that Penzance no longer had the use of Phillimore's old court at Westminster. Since he was given no court room of his own in the new Law Courts in the Strand, he was obliged to sit sometimes in the archbishop's library at Lambeth, and sometimes in a committee room of the House of Lords.

This was the court which Tait hoped would put down the ritualists with the approval of everyone else. At the beginning of 1875 he supposed that even the High Churchmen might accept it. In January he arranged a conciliatory meeting with twelve of their leaders. A week later he invited Liddon and Dean Church to Addington for a 'free talk' on the subject. His point, wrote Church, was 'no legislation: nothing to bring things before Parliament, which does not want to meddle; but

[1] Beaconsfield Papers, B/XII/F/69.

[2] J. G. Hubbard, *Ecclesiastical Courts, a letter to his Grace the Lord Archbishop of Canterbury*, 1880.

[3] To Tait, 13 Nov. 1875, Tait Papers, Misc. Corr., vol. 233, fo. 84.

[4] Hansard, vol. 220, 142.

[5] *The Times*, 20 Nov. 1877.

trust the new Court, and make it as good a Court as you can.'
He disclaimed all designs against the 'great historical High
Church party'.[1] Church began to doubt this when he read the
bishops' declaration of intentions in *The Times*, which seemed
to him, in spite of its appeal for patience on all sides, 'very
much like the exhortation to repent and confess, addressed by
the Inquisition to obstinate heretics, *after* they had delivered
up the patients to the secular arm'. He wrote to his bishop to
say that some of his own practices were clearly under censure
and that he was ready to be prosecuted along with the ritualists.[2]

FIG. 7

'Anything But in Retreat'. The Revd. A. H. Mackonochie defies both
Lord Penzance and the Archbishop of Canterbury.

Other High Churchmen joined in attacking the act. 'I am
no Ritualist myself,' Canon McColl told Tait, 'but I like
justice and fair play.'[3] At this moment the ritualists badly
needed such allies. The attack on ritual, they urged, was really

[1] M. C. Church, *Life of Dean Church*, p. 247.
[2] B. A. Smith, *Dean Church*, 1958, pp. 184 f.
[3] Tait Papers, Misc. Corr., vol. 193, fo. 146.

aimed at the doctrines and practices of the whole High Church party. '*Let us all hold together*', wrote J. B. Dykes.[1] As a result of the Public Worship Regulation Act, the ritualists and High Churchmen set about healing the breach that had developed between them.

The Political Consequences of the Act

On 11 October 1874 a friend told Disraeli, 'You have not a single internal difficulty.' Disraeli commented, 'I hope he is a prophet, but I am not an admirer—at least in politics—of cloudless skies.'[2] Some clouds were already visible. During the debate Dean Duncombe of York had written that the clergy in Yorkshire were so indignant that if a snap general election were to be held, 'not a single Conservative candidate would have the least chance' throughout the country. This was an exaggeration, for during the prosecution of the Revd. S. F. Green under the act, fifty-two Sheffield clergymen sent Green's bishop a letter of support.[3] Nevertheless, numerous High Churchmen had written to Disraeli renouncing their membership of the Conservative party because of his behaviour during the debate. After his speech on 'the Mass in masquerade', one of them wrote that if it indicated the line marked out for Conservatism, 'why then—*To the winds with Conservatism!*'[4]

Disraeli had seriously underestimated the political strength of the ritualists. In 1851 a German observer had spotted that the High Church party consisted of 'gentlemen', concerned with increasing the movement's 'wealth, its authority, and its political influence'.[5] Until 1874 their stance (in line with the rest of the Church of England)[6] was mostly Conservative. But the ritualists had already flexed their political muscles in Rochdale in 1859, when the Member of Parliament, Sir Alexander Ramsay, lost his seat after a speech threatening to

---

[1] Dykes, *Eucharistic Truth*, p. 112.

[2] Cairns Papers, P.R.O. 30/51/1.

[3] G. W. E. Russell, *Malcolm McColl: Memoirs and Correspondence*, 1914, p. 37. H. K. Smith, *William Thomson*, p. 100.

[4] Beaconsfield Papers, B/XII/F/86. Dykes, *Eucharistic Truth*, p. 95.

[5] J. J. Weber, *Illustrierter London-Führer*, Leipzig, 1851, ed. and trans. W. C. Arnstein as 'A German View of English Society: 1851' in *Victorian Studies*, vol. xvi, no. 2, Dec. 1972, p. 202.

[6] J. R. Vincent, *How the Victorians Voted*, 1967; cf. *Armstrong's Norfolk Diary*, ed. H. B. J. Armstrong, 1963, pp. 29 and 76.

throw them out of the Church by the scruff of their necks. When the cheering had subsided, a leading Puseyite remarked, 'Ramsay will never be M.P. for Rochdale any more.'[1] Now Disraeli and Tait had revived the political emotions of the ritualists. The new act, as Bright observed, was aimed at the sons of gentlemen, educated at the ancient universities, 'accustomed to associate with the great wealth and high blood of the peerage'. Such men could be extremely dangerous, and Sir John Gorst prophesied that if Tait continued 'his career of ecclesiastical legislation' the Government would be in great danger of 'being broken up by the High Church party'.[2]

The Government's apparent condonation of the Turkish atrocities against Bulgarian Christians in 1876 gave the ritualists their first chance of revenge. Liddon was the first to attack the Turks, in a sermon preached at St. Paul's, and Pusey sent a letter of blessing to the national anti-Turkish convention held in St. James's Hall.[3] Contemporaries saw this religious agitation as a reprisal for the 1874 act. Bishop Magee said that the clergymen who signed Liddon's declaration against war for Turkey were really signing a 'ritualistic declaration of war with Dizzy to revenge the P.W.R.' And Disraeli himself observed that, in the controversy, dissenting ministers and Liberals had been joined by a 'Hudibrastic crew of High Ritualists'. He said that Lord Carnarvon, who went against the Government now (as in 1874), was unintentionally lending himself 'to a sacerdotal intrigue'.[4]

Among the 455 petitions and memorials on the subject in the Public Record Office, two from Frome in Somerset illustrate precisely the religious and political divisions of the controversy. The Revd. W. E. Daniel, Vicar of Trinity Church, Frome, and Major Wickham, Chairman of the Frome Conservative Association, were the leading signatories of the petition in support of the Government. The first four signatures on the second petition,

[1] J. R. Vincent, *The Formation of the British Liberal Party, 1857–68*, Pelican edn., 1972, p. 150.
[2] J. Bright, *Public Addresses*, ed. J. E. Thorold Rogers, 1879, p. 232, speaking in Birmingham, 25 Jan. 1875. Gorst in Beaconsfield Papers, B/XII/F/81a.
[3] Johnston, *Life of Liddon*, pp. 205–51. A. J. P. Taylor, *The Trouble Makers*, 1957, p. 78 (where Liddon's sermon is misdated).
[4] MacDonnell, *Life of Magee*, ii. 87. Monypenny and Buckle, *Life of Disraeli*, ii. 925 and 968; cf. ibid. 670 and 922 for G. E. Buckle's view.

attacking the Government, were those of the Revd. W. J. E. Bennett, the ritualist Vicar of Frome's main parish church, of his two curates and his churchwarden.[1] Bennett had been appointed to the living by Lord Bath in 1852, and in that year Mr. Daniel and Major Wickham had raised another petition in protest to Bath over the appointment.[2]

The two petitions of 1876 were forwarded to the Foreign Secretary by Mr. H. C. Lopes, Conservative M.P. for Frome since 1874.[3] As a supporter of the Public Worship Regulation Act, Lopes had greatly irritated Bennett, who wrote to Lord Bath in July 1874, 'For ourselves, we shall not care much for Mr. Lopes, unless Mr. Lopes cares for *us*. And he will find us at Froome [*sic*] on the liberal side, I fear.'[4] In the event Bennett and his curates never openly supported the Liberals. Nor did Lord Bath. His opposition to the 1874 act had been, according to Magee, 'particularly spiteful and obstinate',[5] and now, in a speech at Frome, he came out strongly against the Government's Eastern policy.[6] But in spite of pressure from Lord Granville, he refused to join the Liberal party.[7]

Even so, the damage had been done. In November, Lopes was unexpectedly called to the judicial bench. At the subsequent by-election the Liberal candidate, H. B. Samuelson, defeated Sir James Fergusson by 93 votes. Both the *Western Gazette* and Samuelson attributed the victory largely to the agitation over the Bulgarian atrocities.[8]

The agitation would have had no practical effect, either at Frome or throughout the country, had it been promoted by ritualists alone. But the curious political alliances which had opposed the Public Worship Regulation Act were liable to

---

[1] P.R.O., FO 78, *Turkey*, 2555. R. T. Shannon, *Gladstone and the Bulgarian Agitation of 1876*, 1963, p. 175, sets out to minimize the importance of ritualism in the affair; he has, however, failed to notice that there are two petitions from Frome, possibly because they are written on identical paper and bound together (cf. 149 and 150 n. 2).

[2] Bennett Letters, Bath Papers, Longleat; Muniments E.

[3] The *Western Gazette*, 29 Sept. and 6 Oct. 1876. For details of how the petitions were got together, ibid. 15 and 22 Sept. 1876.

[4] Bennett Letters, loc. cit.

[5] MacDonnell, op. cit. ii. 8.

[6] The *Western Gazette*, 6 Oct. 1876, p. 5.

[7] Granville Letters, Bath Papers, Longleat; Muniments E.

[8] The *Western Gazette*, 26 Nov. 1876, where Samuelson's letter to the *Globe* is quoted.

repeat themselves. Gladstone's campaign against the Bulgarian atrocities was directed from Lord Bath's country seat.[1] The radicals and liberationists, who were disgusted by ritual, found themselves once again applauding ritualists.[2] The ritualists possessed enough political capital to make the 'trumperies' temporarily irrelevant. In inviting Lord Bath to support and speak at the Eastern conference of 1876, Lord Westminster wrote that he would be 'very glad if we could get the adhesion of some Conservatives to balance the Radicals'.[3] That was made possible by Disraeli's behaviour in 1874; and the moral fervour with which he was now attacked was the fervour of those who seek revenge.

Ritualists and Socialists

The political attitudes of ritualists and High Churchmen were inevitably affected by the calculation that a government prepared to pass the Public Worship Regulation Act could have no intention of showering them with ecclesiastical honours. Lord Beauchamp told Cairns in 1876 that he had 'always been desirous of checking the attack of the High Church Radicals upon the Conservative Party', but that their behaviour was understandable, provided 'no one suspected of Ritualism is to receive preferment of the slightest kind at the hand of the Government'.[4]

To be cold-shouldered by, if not finally excluded from, the governing classes also affected the social attitudes of ritualist clergymen. Newman and his contemporaries had shared a paternalism that distrusted even reading rooms for working men. Although the early Tractarians hated Erastianism, this led none of them to attack the existing social order; when they were not actually Conservative, they remained carefully neutral in politics.[5] To castigate wealth, as Pusey did, was

---

[1] Taylor, op. cit., p. 80.

[2] The *Northern Echo*, 20 Aug. and 4 Sept. 1876; cf. its leader attacking ritualism, 16 Apr. 1874, p. 2. Its editor, W. T. Stead, said that disestablishment was a minor consideration compared with the England's behaviour in the east: Tait Papers, vol. 96, fos. 194 ff.

[3] Letters on the Eastern Question, Bath Papers, Longleat; Muniments E, 30 Nov. 1876.

[4] Beauchamp to Cairns, 17 Sept. 1876, Cairns Papers, P.R.O. 30/51/19.

[5] Newman's letter to *The Times*, Feb. 1841, in *Newman: Prose and Poetry*, ed. G. Tillotson, 1957, pp. 75 ff. Tractarian political neutrality is examined in J. R.

exceptional (although Pusey's disciple, Dr. W. H. Hook of Leeds, considered himself 'almost a Radical' for believing that bishops should become 'as poor as Ambrose or Augustine, &c. &c., that they may make the people truly rich').[1] Now, however, the victims of religious persecution discovered a new affinity with the victims of the social order. Even before 1874, patrons of ritualists had been few enough; but the personal wealth of their supporters had enabled them to build churches of their own, of necessity in places not cared for by the fashionable churches from which they were excluded. J. G. Hubbard, the city banker who built St. Alban's, Holborn, declared that it existed 'especially for the sake of the poor', because 'rich and poor are alike in the sight of God'. The ritualists hated pew rents; S. F. Green forbade them at Miles Platting and thus, as one of his parishioners said, 'abolished class distinctions, which ought never to be seen in Church'. Even when they were given important livings, the ritualists attacked these symbols of the class system. George Perry-Gore, Vicar of Oldham, said that pew rents had practically excluded the poor from his church and made it 'for all intents and purposes a proprietary chapel of the wealthy and well-to-do middle classes'.[2]

The ritualists soon turned their exclusion from fashionable districts into moral superiority. Before he accepted a living from Lord Bath and became a *habitué* at Longleat, W. J. E. Bennett built for himself St. Barnabas's, Pimlico, which was opened in 1850. He invited the rich to visit the 'dens of infamy, and the haunts of vice, ignorance, filth and atheism', before reading the parable of Dives and Lazarus. 'Then look at your noble houses, and the trappings of your equippages, the gold that glitters on your sideboards, and the jewels that gleam on your bosom.'[3] Under the influence of F. D. Maurice, some of the ritualists began to think that 'the claim of some injured or

Griffin, 'The Radical Phase of the Oxford Movement', *Journal of Ecclesiastical History*, vol. 27, no. 1, Jan. 1976, pp. 47–56.

[1] E. B. Pusey, *The Danger of Riches*, 1850. Hook in Ashwell and Wilberforce, *Life of Wilberforce*, i. 225.

[2] J. G. Hubbard quoted in Reynolds, *Martyr of Ritualism*, p. 91 *Reminiscences, Letters, and Journals of T. P. Heywood, Bart.*, Manchester, 1899, p. 253. G. Perry-Gore, *The Oldham Chapelry*, Oldham, 1906, p. 48.

[3] Quoted in S. G. Evans, *The Social Hope of the Christian Church*, 1965, p. 150.

neglected class' might be even more important than vestments.[1] As Dr. Dieter Voll has shown, these men often combined their love of ritual with an Evangelical fervour to save souls, particularly the souls of slum-dwellers. (Dr. Voll describes Lowder and Mackonochie as 'Patriarchs of the East End Slums and Martyrs for the Ritualist Cause'.[2]) In such a situation it was impossible to ignore social problems or to fail to respond to them, however inadequately. As part of his mission to London Docks, Lowder started a Working Men's Institute, which was enthusiastically supported by Maurice (in spite of his break with Pusey). The Public Worship Regulation Act gave a powerful impetus to all this. The Church of England Working Men's Society, formed in 1876 under the guidance of the E.C.U., grew out of a committee set up to defend Mackonochie against persecution for ritualism and to campaign against the new act. In the same year Bennett started a branch at Frome. By 1880 its membership was 9,500 (including 1,228 'honorary' members who were 'not strictly working men in the ordinary sense of the word').[3]

Having broken with the Conservatives, High Churchmen found it difficult to associate with the class of people who naturally voted Liberal. 'So much for "Church and State"', wrote Archdeacon Denison after the passing of the 1874 act, '. . . and for the Prime Minister who calls upon Churchmen to support his Government.' But instead of joining the Liberal party, Denison became an extreme Tory, thanking heaven that he was 'never a Conservative'.[4] The ritualists found it much easier to associate with working men than with small shopkeepers, and they gave style to the developing Labour movement. The most popular speakers at Labour church meetings—James Adderley, Conrad Noel, Percy Dearmer, and Stewart Head-lam—were all ritualists.[5] In Headlam's thinking, ritualism and socialism were inseparable. In 1877 he founded the Guild of St. Matthew, whose members, he said, 'connected the restoration of the Mass to its proper place with our secular and

---

[1] J. Ll. Davies quoted in Evans, *The Social Hope of the Christian Church*, p. 155.
[2] Voll, *Catholic Evangelicalism*, p. 86 and ch. 3: 'Ritualistic Evangelicalism'.
[3] K. S. Inglis, *The Churches and the Working Classes in Victorian England*, 1963, p. 46.
[4] Denison, *Notes of My Life*, pp. 58 and 69.
[5] Inglis, op. cit., p. 231.

political work'. They were Socialists because they were 'Sacramentarians', he claimed.[1]

Headlam was never beneficed, and after 1882 he did not get another curacy. Mandell Creighton, who gave him a general licence in 1898, was criticized for doing so.[2] Ritualism made Headlam an outsider, and he became a friend to outsiders: as a member of the Fabian Society he led the funeral procession in honour of Alfred Linnell, who was killed when police charged a trades union rally in Trafalgar Square in 1887; he went bail for Oscar Wilde and brought him home after his imprisonment.[3] He once hinted at the connection between these sympathies and the attempt to put down ritualists: the Bishop of London had criticized his friendship for the atheist Walter Bradlaugh and his defence of Bradlaugh's attempts to enter Parliament, and Headlam replied, 'I could hardly expect your Lordship to defend me. Defence, my Lord, is about the last thing which I, myself especially, and any priests who go a little out of the ordinary way in trying to fetch the wanderers home to the flock, have learnt to expect from their bishops.'[4]

In 1904 Headlam appeared before the Royal Commission on Ecclesiastical Discipline. First he apologized for having used a primatial cross in church when no archbishop was present (adding impolitely that the person carrying the cross 'was not unknown to the Archbishop in his youth, and is now a manager at a well conducted music hall').[5] Then Headlam told the commissioners that the real disorders in the Church were 'social and industrial and not ritual, and they are terrible'. Such ritual errors as he may have committed were, he asserted, 'matters of infinitesimal importance compared with the facts that in the London diocese and the Canterbury province, so many little children have no clean beds to sleep on, so many of our dearly beloved brethren have not healthy homes to live

[1] Quoted in *For Christ and the People*, ed. M. B. Reckitt, 1968, p. 71.

[2] Evans, op. cit., p. 176, n. 29. L. Creighton, *Life and Letters of Mandell Creighton*, 1904, ii. 278.

[3] C. Mackenzie, *On Moral Courage*, 1962, ch. iv.

[4] W. L. Arnstein, *The Bradlaugh Case*, 1965, p. 165.

[5] *Report* of the Royal Commission on Ecclesiastical Discipline, 11305. The archbishop in question was Randall Davidson. For Headlam and the Music Hall, see Reckitt, op. cit., pp. 62 and 75–8.

in, so many are out of work, so many are overworked, so many are underpaid.'[1]

The Anglo-Catholic movement, as J. A. Froude observed, was clearly no longer 'Toryism in ecclesiastical costume'. Fr. C. P. Hopkins, for example, who founded in 1899 the Order of St. Paul, a quasi-monastic mission to seamen, firmly supported trade-unionism and socialism.[2] Such a stance was by this time far from exceptional. In 1932, in an often quoted passage, H. D. A. Major attributed to the leadership of Bishop Charles Gore the fact that the Church of England, once regarded as the Tory party at prayer, had become, 'at least in the persons of the Anglo-Catholic clergy, the Socialist party at Mass'.[3] Major was giving Gore credit for a development that had been well under way before the Bishop was ordained.

Church and State

In 1866 Sir Stafford Northcote had told Disraeli that some of the High Churchmen were so alarmed at the danger of Erastianism that they were looking to Gladstone to bring about disestablishment.[4] By the end of 1874 many thought that the moment for it had arrived. Magee heard 'on good authority' that Gladstone was 'fast repining for Disestablishment' after the defeat of his six resolutions. A leading article in the *Liverpool Mercury* said that the intransigence of the ritualists had made disestablishment unavoidable.[5] Many of them rejoiced at the prospect: Liddon approved because it would get the bishops out of the Lords. A change in the election of bishops, wrote a member of the Society of the Holy Cross, was the only possible reparation for the Public Worship Regulation Act, short of its speedy repeal.[6]

Most ritualists were rich enough not to fear the possibility of disendowment along with disestablishment. 'Let the State send forth the Church roofless, and penniless, but free,' said Mackonochie, 'and I will say "Thank you".' He and Stanton

---

[1] *Report* of the Royal Commission on Ecclesiastical Discipline, 11312.

[2] Froude, *Short Studies*, iv. 249. Calder-Marshall, *The Enthusiast*, p. 266.

[3] H. D. A. Major in the *Modern Churchman*, vol. xxi, Feb. 1932, p. 583.

[4] M. Cowling, *1867: Disraeli, Gladstone and Revolution*, 1967, p. 93.

[5] MacDonnell, *Life of Magee*, ii. 10. *Liverpool Mercury*, 18 Sept. 1874, p. 6.

[6] Johnston, *Life of Liddon*, p. 273. *A Vindication from the Bible and the Book of Common Prayer of the Society of the Holy Cross*, by a priest, 1877, p. 41.

had joined Edward Miall's Liberation Society to press for disestablishment in the 1860s, but had resigned shortly afterwards to form, with Archdeacon Denison and others, a 'Church League for promoting the Separation of Church and State'.[1] In 1874, Bennett of Frome welcomed the prospect of Gladstone's joining the Liberationists, now that he was 'reinvigorated by the Catholics'. Tractarian theology had no need of an established church. As Bennett wrote, 'our temporal benefices will be taken away, but our spiritual power will remain'.[2] Since it was also commonly believed that a disestablished church was certain to become more High Church,[3] the ritualists were able to use disestablishment as a threat to their ecclesiastical opponents. In 1885 Dean Oakley of Manchester told the Evangelical Vicar of Kersal that High Churchmen were 'quite strong enough, and *very much tempted* at times, to pull our common house roof down over your heads; and we shall most assuredly do it, rather than let the key pass into your hands again.'[4]

The Liberation Society was naturally delighted at all this. In August 1874 its journal had protested that the Public Worship Regulation Bill had wasted Parliament's time, turning the national assembly into a church synod. Its members shared the ritualists' dislike of the bishops. (One of them publicly accused Tait of offering eight of his relatives preferments worth £8,221 per annum.) The controversy in Parliament enabled them to argue that disestablishment was the remedy for all sides in the dispute over ritualism. In 1876 Joseph Chamberlain, speaking as president of the Society, asserted that 'Persecution, which was not inherent in religion, became imported into it when the State established it.'[5]

Not everyone agreed. Although all ritualists and High Churchmen opposed Erastianism, many were not so sure of the value of disestablishment. Gladstone's own views were equivocal. When Gladstone retired from public life at the end of 1875, his

[1] Reynolds, *Martyr of Ritualism*, pp. 149 and 207.
[2] Bennett Letters, 10 June and 13 July 1874, Bath Papers, Longleat; Muniments E.
[3] e.g. by Magee: MacDonnell, op. cit. ii. 281.
[4] J. Oakley, *Correspondence between Prebendary Macdonald and the Dean of Manchester*, Manchester, 1885, p. 14.
[5] The *Beehive*, 22 Aug. 1874. The *Western Gazette*, 4 Feb. and 12 May 1876.

views were already equivocal, and Lord Blachford was unable to determine whether this was 'a step from or towards his adoption of disestablishment'.[1] 'To say that the Ritualists as a body are in favour of disestablishment is surely a marvellous inaccuracy of speech,' wrote R. J. Wilson in 1874.[2] As time passed some of the ritualists themselves became part of the establishment. When Edward King became a professor in 1873, he said that he was determined to convince 'the young men of Oxford that the Church of England is something more than the shell of an establishment'; but as Bishop of Lincoln, in 1887 he said that the real desire of the ritualists was not disestablishment but 'to maintain the true and legitimate relations between the spiritual and temporal jurisdictions'.[3]

The ritualists' preference for socialism rather than Liberalism helped to minimize the cry for disestablishment. Towards the end of the 1890s, Henry Scott Holland put what he called 'The Radical Case against Disestablishment'. 'We might pronounce Disestablishment', he said, 'to belong to the epoch of the Liberalism of the individual, troubled with an individual conscience and its peevish rights. We might show how we have left this excellent man behind, still explaining his limited, petty woes; and that we have moved on, unable to wait for him, on the stronger elements of the mass (not Popish); swept up with its recognition of the corporate life, and its socialistic humanitarianism, and all that most harmonises with a Church.'[4] Some Anglo-Catholics, as they were now calling themselves, still supported disestablishment.[5] But what most of them wanted, according to one of their chief opponents, was 'a substantive existence, independent equally of State control and of the great Western Communion that looks to Rome for its authority'.[6] This useful stance enabled them both to draw money from the State and to act as its conscience and critic. It seemed to work. Wilhelm Stählin, a German Lutheran who came across Anglo-Catholicism in the early years of the twentieth century, commented that he had never met such notions before, but

---

[1] *Letters of Lord Blachford*, ed. G. E. Marindin, 1896, p. 360.
[2] Wilson, *An Earnest Protest*, p. 11.
[3] Russell, *Edward King*, p. 41. The *Lincoln Diocesan Magazine*, June 1887, p. 19.
[4] *Henry Scott Holland, Memoir and Letters*, ed. S. Paget, 1921, p. 212.
[5] D. C. M. Boycott, *The Secret History of the Oxford Movement*, 1933, p. 163.
[6] E. A. Knox, *Reminiscences of an Octogenarian, 1847–1934*, 1934, p. 302.

'they were planted in me; and they were waiting for their hour'.[1] Stählin became Bishop of Oldenburg and was leading opponent of the Hitler regime during the *Kirchenkampf*, while a good number of other men influenced by British Anglo-Catholics took the same stance.[2] These men made 'fundamental demands for the independence of Church and State whilst still holding fast to the idea of a national church',[3] which Heinrich Hermelinck described as unique to Anglo-Catholicism.

[1] W. Stählin, *Via Vitae, Lebenserrinerungen*, Kassel, 1968, p. 97.

[2] See my article 'British and German High Churchmen in the Struggle against Hitler', *Journal of Ecclesiastical History*, vol. xxiii, no. 3, July 1972, pp. 233–49.

[3] H. Hermelinck, *Das Christentum in der Menschheitsgeschichte von der Französischen Revolution bis zur Gegenwart*, Tübingen, 1953, iii. 259.

V

THE ACT IN OPERATION

Trials and Imprisonments

ONLY two weeks after the new act came into force, the
Church Association persuaded some parishioners of the
district chapelry of St. Peter, Folkestone, to complain
that the incumbent, the Revd. C. J. Ridsdale, was indulging in
twelve objectionable practices. These included the use of vestments and the eastward position. Folkestone lay in Tait's own
diocese, and the Archbishop declined to veto the proceedings,
in the vain hope that Ridsdale, who had given him trouble before, would find acceptable whatever judgement was made
under the new act. Ridsdale refused, and in true ritualist fashion
he said that by appearing before Lord Penzance's court, no one
should suppose that he conceded it any spiritual jurisdiction.
His chief opponent, Mr. Clifton, was represented in court by
A. J. Stephens; as the leading Evangelical lawyer, Stephens
had no doubts about Penzance's competence to try the case,
and indeed was Erastian enough to hold that appeals 'to the
Sovereign in Council were appeals to an Ecclesiastical, not a
Civil Court'.[1]

The case set the pattern for later disputes. The activities of
the Church Association were paralleled by those of the E.C.U.,
which paid Ridsdale's costs and hired Sir James Fitzjames
Stephen as his lawyer. The ritualists sought to blacken their
opponents by accusing Mr. Clifton of being bribed by the
Church Association; they also claimed that he had agreed to
withdraw his testimony in exchange for £200! None of this
affected the outcome of the trial, and Penzance ruled against
Ridsdale on all points. Ridsdale then appealed to the Judicial
Committee of the Privy Council on four of them: the use of
wafer bread, vestments, the eastward position, and a crucifix
and candles on the rood screen. On 12 May 1877 the Privy

---

[1] Ridsdale to Tait, Tait Papers, Misc. Corr., vol. 217, fo. 281. A. J. Stephens,
A Letter to His Grace the Lord Archbishop of York, 1873, p. 10.

Council decided that all four points were unacceptable in the Church of England (conceding that no one could prove that Ridsdale had actually used wafer bread).[1]

Rejecting the Ornaments Rubric as being incomplete in itself, the Privy Council accepted as statutory (under Elizabeth I, c. 2) the Advertisements of 1566, which made an order against the vestments allowed by Edward VI's first Prayer Book. The judgement therefore followed the ruling of the Privy Council in the Purchas case that only surplice, scarf, and hood should be used at all ministrations.

This apparently unanimous and simple decision concealed a deep split in the Privy Council. One of its members, Sir Robert Phillimore, had been Dean of Arches during the Purchas case and had then ruled that vestments, wafer bread, the mixed chalice, and the eastward position were all legal. On appeal, the Privy Council of the time had overruled him (incidentally reversing its own *obiter dictum* in the case of *Westerton* v. *Liddell* that the eastward position was within the law). Phillimore still refused to go against his previous opinions; other members, however, were extremely anxious to stop any private differences amongst the Privy Councillors being made public, which they found difficult. Lord Selborne (who had been reluctant to serve in the case at all)[2] wrote to Cairns that 'the forgetfulness, by one or more of our number, of the obligations (as I understand them,) of the Privy Councillor's oath' was allowing 'unscrupulous parties to do their best (or worst) to discredit the judgement before it is delivered, or at all events to neutralize any tendency which it might have to do good.'[3]

In the end, Cairns himself invoked an Order in Council of 1627 to prevent the minority from expressing its opinion; but Sir Fitzroy Kelly leaked the information that he, Phillimore, and Lord Justice Amphlett (who were not present when the judgement was delivered) had dissented. He added that in his opinion it was a political judgement.[4] Amphlett, a Broad

---

[1] *The Times*, 14 May 1877; cf. *Clifton* v. *Ridsdale*, 1 P.D. 316, 2 P.D. 376. The accusation of bribery was made by the Revd. Matthew Woodward, quoted in C. J. Ridsdale, *The Ridsdale Judgement*, n. d., p. 15.

[2] Selborne to Cairns, 22 Dec. 1876, in Cairns Papers, P.R.O. FO.30/51/9.

[3] Ibid., Selborne to Cairns, 9 Apr. 1877.

[4] Sir F. Kelly in *The Times*, 29 Oct. 1877; J. B. Atley, *The Victorian Chancellors*,

Churchman, regretted the indiscretion, but he told Herbert Paul that Kelly was right: 'It was a flagitious judgement.'[1]

In the judgement itself, however, these differences emerged only in an attempt to mollify High Churchmen over the eastward position: it was ruled that a clergyman could face whichever way he chose at the Eucharist, provided that the act of consecration was visible to the congregation. But High Churchmen were not mollified; their indignation at the judgement matched Low Church jubilation. The Lower House of Convocation responded by recommending, by 41 votes to 5, that the Privy Council allow the use of a cope (with the bishop's consent) at Holy Communion. Wilbraham Egerton felt that the decision was setting aside part of historic Anglicanism; but he urged the ritualists to obey the law whilst they agitated for its repeal. Bishop Selwyn still clung to the hope that the contrary parties in the Church would avoid the law altogether by submitting to their bishops, but he failed to see that the Ridsdale case had made this possibility even less likely than before.[2] Gladstone called the whole affair 'an unjust and unwise prosecution'. Dean Church's response was to draw up a memorial asserting that no authority would be considered binding on clergymen unless it proceeded from the Church as well as the State. This was signed by 77 clergymen—a select group that included four deans, eight archdeacons, thirteen canons, and Tait's own chaplain! (The presence of episcopal assessors at the trial had clearly failed to give the judgement any more spiritual authority in the eyes of these memorialists. Pusey had indeed already told Tait that their presence only made things worse.) As Liddon observed, the Ridsdale case promised to be one of those 'victories which are fatal to the conqueror'.[3]

Behind the scenes, dissension amongst the bishops still blocked Tait's plans. He had decided that the five senior bishops, four of whom were Low Churchmen, should be the episcopal assessors on the Judicial Committee of the Privy

---

ii. 318; R. Phillimore, *The Ecclesiastical Law of the Church of England*, 2nd edn., 1895, ii. 976.

[1] Paul, *History of Modern England*, iv. 352, n. 1.

[2] W. Egerton, *Practical Readjustments of the Relation of the Church to the State*, 1877, p. 8. H. W. Tucker, *The Life and Episcopate of G. A. Selwyn*, 1879, ii. 338.

[3] Gladstone, *Letters*, ii. 182. *Guardian*, 4 Apr. 1877. Liddon, *Life of Pusey*, iv. 283 f. Johnston, *Life of Liddon*, p. 215.

Council. Wordsworth insisted on a meeting of other interested
bishops to discuss the matter. After he had forced Tait's hand
by threatening to reveal all to the general public, four junior
bishops, selected in rotation, were added to Tait's five.[1]

To the regret of the militants, however, Ridsdale had already
given way. His recent marriage, perhaps, made him reluctant
to risk by further disobedience the possible penalties of inhibition[2] or (after three years) voidance of his benefice. After Penzance's judgement he had wavered, announcing his intention
of disobedience while in fact suspending services at St. Peter's
pending the appeal. When the appeal was lost he announced
that his conscience favoured carrying on according to the
rubrics, but he would cease to follow his conscience if Tait (as
his spiritual superior) would dispense him of the sin. Tait readily
agreed and on 7 June he wrote granting Ridsdale 'a complete
dispensation from the obligation under which you believe
yourself to be'.[3]

Tait's success was short-lived. From now on no arraigned
priest ever appeared to stand trial in person before Penzance's
court, even when threatened with imprisonment, and Tait
never again succeeded in persuading a ritualist to accept any
of its judgements. Before the Ridsdale case was decided,
Penzance suspended for three months the Revd. Arthur Tooth,
Vicar of St. James's, Hatcham, in the diocese of Rochester.
The E.C.U. lawyers tried to argue that the trial was unfair
simply because Tooth had refused to appear. In fact Penzance
behaved with great competence, excluding those charges
which were still *sub judice* in the Ridsdale case, and condemning
Tooth only on others which had already been declared illegal
by the Judicial Committee of the Privy Council. Tooth refused
to obey his monition, the formal notice that he should give up
his illegal actions;[4] the E.C.U. proposed that any suspension
or inhibition under the act was '*spiritually* null and void',

[1] Wordsworth to Crauford Tait, 20 Sept. 1876, Tait Papers, Misc. Corr.,
vol. 215, fo. 62; copy of letter from Tait to Cairns, 5 Oct. 1876, ibid., fo. 113.
These assessors were in any case not allowed to say much; see Selborne to Cairns,
9 Apr. 1877, in Cairns Papers, P.R.O. FO.30/51/9.

[2] See Appendix: The Text of the Public Worship Regulation Act, section 13,
pp.137 f. 7.

[3] Copy in Tait Papers, Misc. Corr., vol. 231, fo. 164.

[4] See Appendix: The Text of the Public Worship Regulation Act, section 9,
p. 134.

adding that any priest so sentenced should continue to discharge his spiritual functions, and that the E.C.U. would support him.[1] Dean Church considered Tooth's position legally indefensible but morally correct. The decision, he declared, represented 'a misuse of law such as has never before been known in history'.[2] The Bishop of Rochester sent several curates (including Randall Davidson)[3] to take over the parish, but Tooth prevented them from entering the church. Rochester then ordered the church to be closed: Tooth and his churchwardens prevented this too.

At this point the complainants applied to Penzance to cite Tooth for contempt of court, invoking a statute of 1813 (53 George III c. 127) which carried the penalty of imprisonment. No one had foreseen such a development. Tooth was still under monition, and still refusing to obey it, once breaking into the church through a window in order to celebrate Holy Communion in vestments for a congregation of 300.[4] He was put into Horsemonger Gaol (near London Bridge), to be released when the bishop's nominee had gained entry to St. James's church and taken over the parish.

His imprisonment lasted twenty-eight days and made him a hero and martyr. The complainants themselves applied for his release, and Magee expressed the wish that during 'the extraction of Tooth . . . the Church could be chloroformed for the operation'. A petition in his favour, signed by 1,242 parishioners was presented to the Bishop, and as a public protest against the whole proceedings the president of the E.C.U. resigned his post as Groom of the Prince of Wales's Bedchamber.[5] Disraeli now translated the Bishop of Rochester to the see of St. Albans, and until a new bishop could be consecrated, the case fell into the lap of the luckless Tait, whose attempts to come to terms privately with Tooth failed completely.[6] At this point the E.C.U. lawyers played a masterstroke: the original trial had been delayed because Penzance

---

[1] Liddon, *Life of Pusey*, iv. 286 f.

[2] M. C. Church, *Life of Dean Church*, p. 253.

[3] Lockhart, *Viscount Halifax*, i. 203.

[4] *The Times*, 14 May 1877, p. 6.

[5] MacDonnell, *Life of Magee*, ii. 62; Boycott, *The Secret History of the Oxford Movement*, p. 191; Lockhart, op. cit. i. 205 ff.

[6] *The Times*, 9 and 16 July, 1877.

could find nowhere to hold his court; Tait had finally lent him Lambeth Palace Library, which, as the lawyers pointed out, being south of the Thames, made the whole trial illegal. (The act laid down that trials must take place either in Westminster, the City of London, or the accused's own diocese.) In the autumn of 1877 Chief Justice Cockburn in the court of Queen's Bench confirmed this and restrained further proceedings.

Before fresh ones could be started, Tooth resigned his benefice, courteously declining to prosecute the complainants or Penzance for false imprisonment. 'He claimed that his health was broken. He lived until 1931, directing an orphanage, a nunnery and a home for drunkards.'[1] For these charitable purposes he set up a Community of the Holy Paraclete, two of whose sisters outlived him.[2]

The case enraged would-be prosecutors, and at the same time forced them to proceed with extreme caution. In the same year, 1877, the Bishop of London had incompetently tried to prosecute the Revd. T. Pelham Dale of St. Vedast's, Foster Lane; Dale was inhibited, that is, forbidden to exercise the cure of souls or perform any church service within the diocese; but it was then discovered that the Bishop had transmitted the representation to Tait who had a proprietary interest in St. Vedast's, and the proceedings were quashed. 'The least that could have been expected', said *The Times*, was that the Bishop's new powers 'should not be thrown away by mere negligence'. Instead of Penzance putting down ritualism, wrote Herbert Paul, 'it began to look as if Ritualism was putting down Lord Penzance'.[3] But the Church Association prosecuted afresh, and, when Dale ignored Penzance's suspension, pressed for imprisonment. In October 1880 he was put into Holloway Gaol. Tait publicly censured the Church Association, and Harold Browne wrote asking Magee how they could get Dale out again: Magee had nothing to suggest.[4] Dale was finally released on Christmas Eve with the help of a habeas corpus, after forty-nine days in prison. This was enough for Dale; he gave in

---

[1] Marsh, *The Victorian Church in Decline*, p. 229.
[2] P. F. Anson, *The Call of the Cloister*, 2nd edn., 1964, p. 529.
[3] *The Times*, 14 July 1877, p. 3; Paul, op. cit. iv. 354.
[4] Tait in *The Times*, 13 Nov. 1880; MacDonnell, op. cit. ii. 144-5.

and accepted a new living in Berkshire,[1] the gift of Christopher Wordsworth.

Already the act seemed to be such an embarrassing failure that, as the Revd. T. T. Carter observed, the bishops were being 'driven to look for some form of personal government' instead.[2] After the failure of the first prosecution of Dale, Bishop Jackson tried to persuade him to retire on £200 a year, dwelling on the vicar's age (he was sixty), 'very much to Mrs. Pelham Dale's indignation'.[3] Dale refused; but some of the Tractarian bishops managed to make 'deals' with their ritualist clergy. Selwyn allowed the Revd. C. Bodington, Vicar of St. Andrew's, Wolverhampton, to do what he liked in church, provided that he also agreed to conduct lawful services for any parishioners desiring them. Tait privately approved.[4] Dean Church did not: if the ritualists made concessions, even to friendly bishops, the real issues would never be faced. When the Church Association attempted to prosecute the Revd. T. T. Carter, Bishop Mackarness asked Carter to assent to his ruling independently of the courts, as if the Judicial Committee of the Privy Council did not exist. Church wrote to dissuade the rector: 'I do not think that a Bishop has a right to urge an Ordination vow in order to force us to agree with him. The very question at issue is, what is the real law, and no single Bishop can claim to rule that.'[5]

The Church Association was equally unwilling to grant the bishops any discretion, even though the act allowed this. In 1878 eight suits were initiated, of which seven were vetoed. To get round this, the Association decided to prosecute Carter under the Church Discipline Act of 1840, but Mackarness still refused to institute a suit. Carter's opponent applied to the Queen's Bench for a *mandamus* to force the Bishop to institute. Mackarness appeared in person to defend himself, and lost, but

[1] *The Life and Letters of T. P. Dale*, ed. his daughter H. P. Dale, 1894, ii. 82. The Archdeacon of Lincoln refused to institute, and this was done by the rural dean.
[2] T. T. Carter, *The Present Movement a True Phase of Anglo-Catholic Church Principles*, 1878, p. 49.
[3] Dale, op. cit. ii. 76.
[4] Tucker, op. cit. ii. 341–9. Tait Papers, letter of 19 Nov. 1877, Misc. Corr., vol. 228, fos. 109 f.
[5] W. H. Hutchings *Life and Letters of T. T. Carter*, 1903, p. 152.

the Lords reversed the judgement and granted him costs.[1] This decision made the bishop's veto impregnable, even though the timid Carter decided he had been through enough and resigned to avoid any further trouble.[2]

If bishops were now willing to make deals with ritualists, the Church Association remained implacable. Its next victim was the Revd. R. W. Enraght, Vicar of Holy Trinity, Bordesley. Enraght had publicly defended the eastward position, adoration of the Blessed Sacrament, prayers for the dead, and auricular confession in a pamphlet which told 'Archbishops, Bishops, Ministers of State and others—who have unhappily departed from the principles of the faithful Bishops and Divines of 1662' —that 'Catholic minded Churchmen, and they only, truly represent the mind of the English Church'.[3] In 1878 Bishop Philpott objected to Enraght's use of altar lights, vestments, the sign of the cross, and the commixture, even though he conceded that Enraght was following customs he had inherited from his predecessor at Holy Trinity.[4] When Enraght refused to give them up, the Bishop allowed him to be prosecuted.

Enraght said he declined to be 'trampled on by the Church Association'; but in July 1879 Convocation revised the Ornaments Rubric, recommending that vestments should not be used contrary to the monition of the diocesan bishop. Enraght believed that this decision gave spiritual authority to the Bishop's earlier requests, and he immediately obeyed them. Although it was now too late for Philpott to apply the veto, both he and Tait urged the complainants and the Church Association to withdraw the suit.[5] They refused, and Penzance condemned Enraght on sixteen counts. Since in Enraght's opinion Penzance had no spiritual authority whatsoever, the Vicar refused to obey his monition: in November 1880, at the Church Association's request, he was put into Warwick Gaol, and in January 1881, on the technical grounds that the writs had not been opened

---

[1] *Julius* v. *Bishop of Oxford*, L.R. 5, Appeal Cases 214–48.
[2] Hutchings, op. cit., pp. 150–1.
[3] R. W. Enraght, *Who are true Churchmen and Who are Conspirators?*, n. d., Dedication and p. 27.
[4] R. W. Enraght, *A Pastoral to the Faithful Worshippers at Holy Trinity, Bordesley*, 1879, p. 5 and *My Ordination Oaths . . . Am I keeping them?*, 1880, pp. 6 and 26.
[5] Marsh, op. cit., p. 266.

in the presence of justices of the Queen's Bench, his imprison-ment was invalidated. He continued his ritualistic practices at Bordesley for another two years, when Philpott inhibited him from serving in his parish.[1]

In 1874 the *Quarterly Review* had declared that it would be difficult to conceive of a measure 'less like a tool of persecution' than the Public Worship Regulation Bill.[2] Now that this unexpected character of the legislation had been revealed, those who had professed themselves to be 'fair and equitable' in 1874[3] were given the opportunity to prove their claim. One of them was James Fraser, Bishop of Manchester.

The Miles Platting Case

James Fraser was in many ways an outstanding bishop. Because of his mastery of educational problems, Gladstone had sent him to Manchester in 1870 when it was 'the centre of the modern life of the country'.[4] He took the place by storm, im-pressing businessmen and working men alike. He arbitrated between master painters and their men in 1874 and 1875, and when the cotton strike of 1878 had continued for seven weeks the operatives referred the disputed points to him, although in the event the employers refused his arbitration. During the fifteen years of his episcopate he spent £31,535 on private charity.[5] An admirer described him as 'one of the most lovable, simple-minded ministers of the Gospel, with whom it was pos-sible to come into contact'.[6]

This description implies a limitation. As James Bryce ob-served, 'He was not a great reader, and had no time for sus-tained and searching thought.' Dean Church (who had been senior to Fraser in Oriel College Senior Common Room, and examined him for his Fellowship) confirmed this judgement. And in the opinion of Matthew Arnold, Fraser 'represented the

[1] R. W. Enraght, *My Prosecution under the Public Worship Regulation Act*, Birming-ham, 1883, pp. 14 and 31.
[2] *Quarterly Review*, Oct. 1874, p. 580.
[3] Fraser, *A Charge delivered at his Primary Visitation*, p. 72.
[4] T. Hughes, *James Fraser, Second Bishop of Manchester*, 1887, pp. 167–8.
[5] Ibid., pp. 226 ff. and 253.
[6] L. M. Hayes, *Reminiscences of Manchester from the Year 1840*, Manchester, 1905, p. 348.

high-and-dry Church . . . with an admixture of the world . . . of the ascetic and speculative side, nothing.'[1] Straightforward Christianity of this kind earned him the admiration of many Anglicans and Nonconformists, and the title of Bishop of All Denominations, but was remote from the preoccupations of contemporary ritualists. Their beliefs, he said, were not Catholic at all 'but mediaeval' and 'certainly not the faith of our age—at least the muscular, rational faith'.[2]

In addition, Manchester had provoked Fraser's latent hostility to Roman Catholicism. The Roman Catholic diocese of Salford, founded in 1850, took in the diocese of Manchester and sheltered perhaps 196,000 Irish Catholic immigrants.[3] Many of these had been exposed for a long time to lower- and middle-class prejudice. Suffering from economic discrimination, they sought in their religion 'a source of unity and an emotional escape from the deprivation of their ghettos'.[4] They also stimulated Orange bigotry. Fraser once said that if he could, he would make 'every Roman Catholic and Nonconformist a full member of the Church of England tomorrow';[5] but it is doubtful whether he meant it. He told his diocesan conference that he could conceive of no branch of the Catholic Church that had departed so widely from Catholic principles as the Church of Rome, and he speculated whether the Council of Nicea 'would have recognized a Bishop of Manchester, and across the water a Bishop of Salford'. Rome he described as the highest example of 'that gigantic system of spiritual domination . . . which some, I fear, are more or less endeavouring to introduce into the Church of England'.[6]

Unfortunately for Fraser, just such endeavours were being made by the Dean of his own cathedral, Benjamin Cowie, who was successfully converting the canons to the eastward position, and was propagating such notions as 'absolution', 'Catholic

---

[1] Bryce, *Studies in Contemporary Biography*, p. 204. R. W. Church, *Occasional Papers*, 1897, ii. 376. Hughes, op. cit., p. 34.

[2] *Daily Courier*, 6 Apr. 1874, p. 8.

[3] A. McCormack, 'Cardinal Vaughan—The Fourth Cardinal', in *Dublin Review*, no. 506, Winter 1965, p. 309.

[4] J. Werly, 'The Irish in Manchester, 1832-49', in *Irish Historical Studies*, vol. xviii, no. 71, Mar. 1973, p. 350.

[5] Hughes, op. cit., pp. 320-1.

[6] J. W. Diggle, *The Lancashire Life of Bishop Fraser*, 1889, pp. 165 and 27.

Practices', and 'the Sacrifice of the Mass' at the diocesan conference.[1] Cowie believed that 'the vile contempt for sacred things in our blessed Protestant times' had wrought havoc in the Church.[2] At the beginning of 1877 he invited W. J. Knox-Little to preach at the Cathedral, and he also set up a ritualist mission in Manchester. Fraser alluded to Knox-Little's visit in a sermon on 'true and false sacerdotalism' shortly before the mission began. He was saddened that 'apparently conscientious men' could think that the truth as it is in Jesus was 'involved in vestments, in the biretta, in acolytes, in purple cassocks'; in his view 'silence, quietness, and the recesses of a man's own heart' were 'the places where the great spiritual work is done, without any parade, without any ostentation, without any cant'. In a private letter he confessed that 'There are a number of men of the extreme school—Mackonochie, Lowder, Bodington and others, who will be here, and in the present state of excitement I can hardly tell what they may say or do.'[3]

These tensions produced disastrously contradictory behaviour. In 1876 the Bishop had warned his diocese that 'if an explosion occurred' as a result of the Public Worship Regulation Act 'no one could anticipate the amount of mischief that might be done'. A train had been laid 'to which any foolish or ill-disposed hand might place a match'.[4] Yet he himself allowed the match to be applied. Once he had made his decision to allow the Act to be used in his diocese, the Bishop was too big a man to go back on it.

In November 1874 he had told 600 of his clergy that he basically approved of the act, even though some people regarded it as tainted by the secular courts. 'I hardly think that anyone present holds that view of their obligations', he said. He could speak the more confidently in so far as at the beginning of the year he had refused to ordain Mr. Harry

---

[1] According to the attack on his views in *Liberalism and the Priest's Craft*, by an Elected Lay Representative, Manchester, n. d., pp. 7, 23, and 28–9. For the eastward position in the cathedral see J. M. Elvey, *Recollections of the Cathedral and Parish Church of Manchester*, Manchester, 1913, p. 27.

[2] Letter quoted in W. Queckett, *My Sayings and Doings*, 1888, p. 22.

[3] Diggle, op. cit., pp. 73–4.

[4] J. Fraser, *A Charge delivered at his Second Visitation*, 1876, p. 7.

Cowgill as Curate of St. John's, Miles Platting, precisely because Cowgill held such an opinion.[1]

Fraser had already clashed with the Rector of St. John's, the Revd. S. F. Green. In 1871 Green had truculently agreed to stop using the mixed chalice, 'at any rate for the present'. He began again two years later,[2] and by 1876 he had introduced vestments and auricular confession into St. John's.[3] In 1877 he explained to the Bishop that he was using incense, not for doctrinal reasons, but to counter 'the effluvia from the chemical works'. By this time Cowgill (who had been ordained by Selwyn of Lichfield) had begun work in Miles Platting, though without Fraser's licence.[4] The Bishop was now under pressure from several of Green's parishioners to stop the Rector's ritualistic practices (for the great majority of his supporters came from outside the parish):[5] in accepting the living in 1869, Green had made it clear that he expected opposition from Orangemen; now a member of the Order, George McDonagh, tried for election as churchwarden.[6]

McDonagh lost the election. The following May he sent Fraser a petition of 320 signatures demanding action against Green. Fraser rejected it, pointing out that whole groups of signatures were in one hand. McDonagh replied that the petitioners were 'but a body of working men, without the means of putting the Public Worship Regulation Act into force', and that their only alternative was to place the matter in the hands of the Church Association.[7]

On 2 December 1878 a presentation by three parishioners, arranged by the Church Association, accused Green of illegally introducing the following into Miles Platting Church:

  i. the mixed chalice;
  ii. altar candles;
  iii. vestments;
  iv. kneeling during the Consecration;

[1] Diggle, op. cit., pp. 160 and 399.
[2] Ibid., p. 398.
[3] H. E. Sheen, 'The Oxford Movement in a Manchester Parish: The Miles Platting Case', unpublished M.A. thesis, Manchester, 1941, p. 95.
[4] Diggle, op. cit., pp. 398–400.
[5] Sheen, op. cit., p. 4, and Tait's Diary, Tait Papers, 26 Feb. 1882.
[6] Heywood, *Reminiscences, Letters, and Journals*, p. 141. Sheen, op. cit., pp. 95 ff.
[7] Hughes, op. cit., pp. 257 f.

v. the elevation of the paten and chalice;
vi. alms placed on the credence table and not the Holy Table;
vii. the sign of the cross;
viii. consecration out of sight of the congregation;
ix. a ceremoniously raised chalice during the service;
x. a brass cross on a ledge above the altar;
xi. a baldacchino.

Fraser asked Green to give up vestments and the mixed chalice. Green refused, and asked the bishop to veto the proceedings. Fraser answered: 'How can I suspend an Act of Parliament in my diocese *meo mero motu*? That's not what my discretion means.'[1]

On 30 December a memorial signed by 208 petitioners (of whom only a quarter lived in Green's parish) asked Fraser to exercise his veto, but it was now too late for this.[2] In June 1879 the case came before Penzance; Green refused to appear or obey a monition forbidding the rituals, and on 9 August Penzance issued an inhibition which Green ignored. In November 1880 the Rector was found guilty of contumacy and contempt of court. The writ *de contumace capiendo* was issued on 9 March 1881, and on 19 March Green was taken to Lancaster Gaol. Cowgill carried on at Miles Platting.

Widespread Revulsion

As Dean Burgon regretfully observed, Green's plight 'attracted extraordinary attention'.[3] It enabled Roman Catholics to mock the Church of England as hopelessly divided and unprincipled. Pusey invited the Church Association to prosecute him for doing what Green had done in church, and Knox-Little almost forfeited a canonry of Worcester because of his violent attack on the imprisonment.[4] Burgon, who abhorred what he called the 'solemn foppery' and 'effete mediaevalism' of the ritualists, lamented that they insisted on going to prison instead

[1] Diggle, op. cit., p. 402; Hughes, op. cit., p. 259.
[2] Hughes, op. cit., p. 260.
[3] J. W. Burgon, *Canon Robert Gregory, a letter of friendly Remonstrance*, 1881, p. 5.
[4] G. H. Castree, *The Rev. Fr. Anderton, S.J., on the Miles Platting Case*, Manchester, 1883, preface. Liddon, *Life of Pusey*, iv. 336. B. A. Smith, *Dean Church*, pp. 204 f.

of simply resigning their livings.[1] But Green was determined to use his imprisonment to humiliate his prosecutors. The Church Association had overreached itself. As Herbert Paul said, it might be just to deprive a clergyman of his living if he disobeyed his bishop and the courts of the land, but 'That he should be put in prison and kept there for the rest of his life, is scandalous, and absurd.'[2] Moreover, if anyone supposed that Green's life in Lancaster Gaol might be fairly comfortable, the Revd. T. P. Dale was at hand to remind men that 'Prison is prison . . . and that means something very disagreeable and unpleasant.'[3]

Fraser, however, was as determined as Green not to give way. He rejected a memorial from the clergy of his diocese for the Rector's release, although he allowed Archbishop Thomson to write asking Green to submit. Green replied that he had read Thomson's letter three times, and concluded that it 'only recommends the course which—as I believe on good grounds— I rejected two and a half years ago.' Both archbishops suggested that if Fraser put a clergyman other than Cowgill in charge of Miles Platting, Green could be safely let out; but the Bishop unconditionally refused their advice, preferring to wait another year until (under the terms of the act) the living would become void. All he agreed to do was write again to Green asking for concessions; Green refused to make any.[4]

During the course of this correspondence Green insisted that he still remained loyal to his canonical oath of obedience to the Bishop. Fraser erroneously supposed this to be a concession, and forwarded Green's letter to Gladstone (who was now Prime Minister). Gladstone was pleased to point out that the royal prerogative of pardon was a matter for the Home Secretary, Sir William Harcourt, to whom the correspondence was now passed. These negotiations were still in progress when Dean Cowie brought before the Manchester diocesan conference a provocative resolution in favour of vestments. In summing up this debate in the conference Fraser revealed that he had lately received a letter indicating that Green was now ready to obey

---

[1] Burgon, op. cit., list of contents, and pp. 47 and 69.
[2] Paul, *History of Modern England*, iv. 353.
[3] Dale, *Life of T. P. Dale*, ii. 93.
[4] Hughes, *James Fraser*, pp. 261–6.

him; however, Green immediately wrote to disabuse him of this error, and the negotiations came to an end.[1] The following September Gladstone tried to exert further pressure on Harcourt by asking whether Green could be released on medical grounds. Harcourt replied, 'What is one to do with a martyr who gains 9lbs in weight in his bondage?' adding acidly, 'I suppose he is denied the opportunities of emaciation which he enjoys when at large'.[2]

On 16 August 1882 Green's benefice became void according to the Public Worship Regulation Act, and Tait asked Gladstone to try to secure his release. Gladstone replied that he and his colleagues were baffled by the legal difficulties.[3] Tait now put pressure on Fraser, who waited until Lord Chancellor Selborne agreed that Green was no longer Rector of St. John's before applying to Penzance for the imprisoned clergyman's release. The promoters of the suit made no objection to the request, and on 4 November 1882 the martyr was set free.[4]

Fraser's campaign against the ritualists was not over, although meanwhile he had allowed Cowgill to run the services at St. John's, whether out of 'kindly inconsistency' or fear of a tumult.[5] Now Sir T. P. Heywood, as patron of the living, nominated Cowgill as rector (Green having ostentatiously resigned rather than allow that Parliament could dismiss an incumbent). Fraser declared that Cowgill was unacceptable and refused to institute him; the Queen's Bench overruled the patron, and the Bishop appointed the Revd. T. Taylor Evans.[6] In 1890 the Revd. Arthur Anderton became rector and revived everything for which Green was imprisoned.[7] The Royal Commission on Ecclesiastical Discipline in 1906 found in use at Miles Platting the commixture, sign of the cross, elevation, altar lights, eastward position, a crucifix and tabernacle, vestments, and wafer bread.[8] When Green died in 1915 the parishioners put a brass plate in St. John's 'to our

[1] Hughes, *James Fraser*, pp. 266–70.
[2] A. G. Gardiner, *Life of Sir William Harcourt*, 1923, i. 384 f.
[3] Gladstone to Tait, Tait Papers, Misc. Corr., 17 Aug. 1882.
[4] Diggle, *Life of Fraser*, pp. 416 f.
[5] Ibid., pp. 407 and 415.
[6] Hughes, op. cit., pp. 275 and 283.
[7] S. Baring-Gould, *The Church Revival*, 1914, p. 250.
[8] *Report* of the Royal Commission on Ecclesiastical Discipline, 1906, 7555.

beloved Rector', inscribed with the text 'He fought the good fight'. The vestments, altar cross, altar lights, and baldacchino remained at Miles Platting until 1973, when the diocesan authorities declared the church redundant and demolished it.

The four imprisonments had changed public opinion. Particularly horrifying had seemed the enforced sale of Green's goods and chattels to pay the legal costs of his opponents (especially since this apparently involved turning on to the streets his wife and five children, the eldest of whom was only six).[1] Sir T. P. Heywood described it in *The Times* as an 'outrage',[2] although in fact, nearly everything Green wished to keep was bought by the E.C.U. and given back to him, along with £222 towards his legal expenses. (The E.C.U. similarly defrayed Dale's legal expenses in 1877, and repaid the rents which were seized to pay the legal costs in his case.[3])

None the less the spectacle was distasteful. 'The exterminating party', said Pusey, had 'run too wild a race'. The Evangelical historian, G. R. Balleine, admitted that 'the brilliant tactics of the Ritualists had won at every point'. The Hon. J. C. Dundas declared that although he had voted for the Public Worship Regulation Act in 1874, he was now horrified at the way it outraged civil and religious liberty; the Evangelical *Record* concluded that litigation was harming the Evangelicals more than the ritualists, and the Revd. J. G. Rogers of the Liberation Society prophesied that the act would 'sink into disuse amid deserved contempt'.[4]

In 1877 Henry Scott Holland had been alarmed at the general and intense hatred shown to ritualists. Now it was felt that to expel them from the Church would 'drive out not only some of the ablest and most devoted of its ministers, but also a very considerable, and to all appearance an increasing, number of the lay members of its communion'. The prolonged resistance of the ritualists, said the *Pall Mall Gazette*, had brought the

[1] Sheen, 'The Oxford Movement in a Manchester Parish . . .', p. 6, and Eccles. Discipline *Report*, p. 70, para. 378.

[2] Heywood, *Reminiscences, Letters and Journals*, p. 150.

[3] Sheen, op. cit., p. 122, and Dale, op. cit. ii. 92–3.

[4] Liddon, op. cit., iv. 370. Balleine, *A History of the Evangelical Party*, p. 232. Dundas in the *York Herald*, 17 Mar. 1882. The *Record*, 14 Nov. 1884, quoted by G. K. A. Bell, *Randall Davidson, Archbishop of Canterbury*, 1935, i. 471. J. G. Rogers, *Antagonism and Litigation in the Established Church*, 1883, p. 11.

alteration or tacit abrogation of the Public Worship Regulation Act 'within the range of practical politics'.[1] Two attempts to change it had already been made. In 1881 Lord Beauchamp presented a bill providing for the automatic release after six months of any clergyman imprisoned in ecclesiastical cases for contempt of court. The following year Archbishop Thomson devised a bill providing for the release of such a clergyman if the archbishop of the province declared that his imprisonment was causing scandal. In both cases, when the Commons came to debate the bill, fewer than forty members were present and the House was counted out.[2]

Even Archbishop Tait now admitted that the act was a failure. His attitude had been changed not so much by the resistance of the ritualists as by the death first of his son and then of his wife. 'When I think of the days of the Public Worship Regulation Act,' wrote Gladstone, 'I can hardly believe him to be the same man.'[3] Tait had come to believe that there should be 'as little interference as possible' in churches where the parishioners were satisfied with the ritual and 'where hearty work is being done', even though in some respects the incumbent might be stretching the law 'beyond its proper limits'.[4] He vetoed the prosecution of Fr. C. F. Lowder, Vicar of St. Peter's, London Docks, explaining to Frederick Temple that he had 'looked into the man's work' and 'would not go on with the prosecution, or allow it'.[5] At the end of 1880, in a speech to the deanery of Wisbere, Kent, he asked for advice on the ritualist problem. Dean Church presented a memorial signed by 5,000 clergymen asking for toleration, but almost as many signed a counter-memorial; Randall Davidson said that one-third of the existing clergy must have signed one or other of these memorials.[6] J. G. Talbot suggested that Tait ask the Cabinet to set up a royal commission on ecclesiastical judicature.[7] Since such a procedure would avoid another full-scale

[1] *Henry Scott Holland, Memoir and Letters*, ed. S. Paget, p. 92. *Pall Mall Gazette*, 19 Jan. 1883.

[2] Hansard, vol. 265, 806–7; vol 269, 812.

[3] Letter to Pusey in Liddon, op. cit., iv. 364.

[4] Memorandum on Ritual Difficulties, 16 Dec. 1880, in Tait Papers, Misc. Corr., vol. 100, fos. 177 f.

[5] *Memoirs of Archbishop Temple*, ed. E. G. Sandford, 1906, ii. 102.

[6] Eccles. Discipline *Report*, 12943–4.

[7] Marsh, *The Victorian Church in Decline*, pp. 268 and 324.

parliamentary debate on the subject, Tait readily agreed, managing to win over to the proposal Gladstone, Disraeli, and Lord Salisbury. In March 1881 the Lords agreed to his own motion for a commission.

Gladstone selected the commission's twenty-five members. Alongside opponents of the ritualists such as Thomson and Penzance, he put High Churchmen such as E. W. Benson and Sir Robert Phillimore. He also included two historians, E. A. Freeman and William Stubbs. Chaired by Tait, the commission began work in May and interviewed fifty-six witnesses. It proposed entirely new courts, distinguishing doctrinal and ritual cases from cases of misconduct; ritual matters were to be tried by the archbishop or bishop, along with his theological and legal assessors, and the final court was to consist of five lay judges, all of whom must be members of the Church of England. The Public Worship Regulation Act was to be repealed.

The commission demonstrated the weight of the case against the act. And the five learned appendices contributed by Stubbs showed that the claims of the ritualists were far more solidly based in English church history than many had supposed.[1] But it was impossible for such a diverse body to present a sufficiently united report on which Parliament could act: only nine members signed without reservation, and Penzance put in a separate report. None of the commission's recommendations became law; the ritualist conflict was not over, and the Public Worship Regulation Act remained.

Bell Cox and Bishop King

Whilst negotiations for the commission were in progress, Bishop Ryle of Liverpool suspended proceedings which had been initiated against the Revd. James Bell Cox, Vicar of St. Margaret's, Toxteth Park.[2] No one expected them to be taken up again. But Ryle—Disraeli's last episcopal appointment —was an anachronism, keeping alive the controversies of the 1870s. A leading Evangelical and former member of the

---

[1] *Report* of the Royal Commission on Ecclesiastical Courts, Parliamentary Papers, 1883, xxiv.

[2] M. L. Loane, *John Charles Ryle, 1816–1900*, 1953, p. 50.

Church Association,[1] he had already been nominated as Dean of Salisbury in 1880, when Disraeli 'in the nick of time'[2] suggested him as Bishop of Liverpool, explaining to Queen Victoria that the gift should be his because the Tories had subscribed the whole of the endowment of the new see and built the bishop's palace. Lord Sandon also urged the Queen to accept Ryle's nomination, saying that his seat for Liverpool depended on a Tory appointment.[3] Ryle arrived in Liverpool to an Orange welcome, and although he was given a cope and mitre for his consecration, he returned them with thanks, declining to make a 'guy of himself'.[4]

Ryle was convinced that the ritualists had 'corrupted, leavened, blinded, and poisoned the minds of many Churchmen' by familiarizing them with 'every distinctive doctrine and practice of Romanism'. However zealous such men might be, they needed extirpating, come what may: 'we ought to stand firm, and to abide the consequences whatever they might be, whether secession, disestablishment, or disruption.'[5] Ryle agreed that the Public Worship Regulation Act had failed; but what he wanted was a better instrument to hammer the ritualists. He hoped that the commission would recommend something other than imprisonment for contempt of court in ritual cases only because 'a surer way of enlisting public support on behalf of a defeated litigant' than the present system 'could not possibly be devised'.[6] When the report was published he was bitterly disappointed. It had failed to sweep away the Ornaments Rubric. If its proposals were sanctioned and became law, he said, there would be 'no more peace in the Church of England'.[7]

---

[1] Baring-Gould, *The Church Revival*, p. 194.

[2] Loane, op. cit., p. 47.

[3] R. B. Walker, 'Religious Changes in Liverpool in the 19th Century', *Journal of Ecclesiastical History*, vol. xix, no. 2, Oct. 1968, p. 198.

[4] *Letters of Queen Victoria*, iii. 78. R. B. Walker, loc. cit. Loane, op. cit., p. 49. Gladstone very much disapproved of the appointment: D. W. R. Bahlman in *Victorian Studies*, p. 356, n. 24.

[5] J. C. Ryle, *Principles for Churchmen*, 4th edn., 1900, p. xx; *A Charge, No. 1*, delivered at his primary Visitation, 1881, pp. 73 and 46. Peter Toon puts a favourable gloss on Ryle's attitudes and actions in 'J. C. Ryle and Comprehensiveness', *Churchman*, vol. 89, no. 4, Oct.–Dec. 1975, esp. pp. 281 and 283 n. 3.

[6] J. C. Ryle, *Address on the Report of the Ecclesiastical Courts Commission*, 1883, p. 4; *A Charge, No. 2, delivered at his Primary Visitation*, 1881, p. 23.

[7] Ryle, *Address on the . . . Commission*, pp. 15–16.

In 1885 complaints were again laid against Bell Cox. Ryle asked him to give up thirteen ritual acts which had been condemned by the Judicial Committee of the Privy Council. The Vicar refused, arguing that canonical obedience was due to no bishop when he was obeying such a court or indeed acting in any way outside his discretion.[1] Ryle refused to exercise the veto, which he held to be both 'indefensible in theory' and 'intolerable in practice',[2] and the case was referred to Penzance. Following ritualist tradition, Bell Cox refused to recognize the court or heed its monition and he was put in Walton Gaol on 4 May 1887. On 20 May the Queen's Bench quashed his conviction on the technical ground that Penzance had pronounced sentence through a proxy.[3]

The proceedings outraged High Churchmen. The new Dean of Manchester, J. Oakley, said that the prosecution was 'far more dangerous to the Established Church than any of her outer foes'. Dean Church told the Archbishop of Canterbury that the case offended his sense of justice much more than had any of the other imprisonments. 'They were in the thick of battle, and of hot blood. This comes after all has cooled down.'[4] Church found a sympathetic ear: Tait had died in 1882, and it was generally felt that the accession of E. W. Benson as his successor marked a new departure in the ritualist controversy, for he had studied these matters all his life.[5] Ryle and his circle, however, had their doubts, both about Benson[6] and about a number of newly appointed and highly suspect bishops. Lord Alwyne Compton, for instance, who had led the clergy of the Southern Convocation in opposition to the act of 1874, was now Bishop of Ely. He made it plain that he did not consider it his duty 'to enquire into minute points of the manner of performing the services'.[7] Wordsworth had been replaced at Lincoln by another ritualist bishop, Edward King, formerly principal of

---

[1] J. B. Cox, *Correspondence between . . . the Bishop of Liverpool and the Revd. J. Bell Cox*, p. 6.

[2] Loane, op. cit., p. 51.

[3] Baring-Gould, op. cit., pp. 252 f.

[4] J. Oakley, *Correspondence between Prebendary Macdonald and the Dean of Manchester*, p. 9. M. C. Church, *Life of Dean Church*, p. 323.

[5] Eccles. Discipline *Report*, 12944 (s).

[6] J. C. Ryle, *Opening Address, Diocesan Conference*, 1883, pp. 5–6.

[7] F. C. Kempson, *The Church in Modern England*, 1908, p. 211.

the High Church theological college at Cuddesdon and the first bishop since the Reformation to wear a mitre.[1] In June 1887 King told the readers of his diocesan magazine that he was sure that all of them would have been grieved at Bell Cox's imprisonment and relieved by his release. 'It is love and loyalty to our Blessed Lord', he added, 'which makes real Church people so keen to act and ready to suffer.'[2] He himself was to be the Church Association's next and final victim.

In 1878, as professor of pastoral theology at Oxford, King had preached for an hour and a quarter against Dean Stanley's attack on auricular confession.[3] In 1881 he had signed Dean Church's address to Tait pleading for tolerance in ritual matters, and as Bishop of Lincoln he had already vetoed one prosecution.[4] The complainant in this case, a solicitor named Ernest de Lacy Read, now determined that the only remedy was to prosecute the Bishop himself. On 4 December 1887 King celebrated the 8 a.m. Eucharist at the reconsecration of the enlarged church of St. Peter-at-Gowts, Lincoln, following the customary ritual of the Vicar. Read petitioned the Arch-bishop of Canterbury to put the Bishop on trial for using altar lights, the commixture, the eastward position, the sign of the cross, the ceremonial ablutions at the end of the service, and for including the Agnus Dei.

Read was a churchwarden at Cleethorpes, and needed support for his petition from within the parish of St. Peter. According to the High Churchman G. W. E. Russell (on the doubtful evidence of a very old friend of a friend's father), the Church Association offered a churchwarden of St. Peter's £1,000 if he would prosecute King, while J. G. Lockhart says that the bribe was £10,000. Contemporary evidence, however, is that 'several persons, including the late parish warden at St. Peter-at-Gowts, were interviewed by agents of the Church Association, but refused to take part in such proceedings.'[5]

---

[1] O. Chadwick, *Edward King, Bishop of Lincoln 1885–1910*, Lincoln, 1968, p. 16.

[2] *Lincoln Diocesan Magazine*, June 1887, pp. 18 and 19.

[3] Described by A. E. Housman in a letter to his father, 12 Feb. 1878, in *The Letters of A. E. Housman*, ed. H. Maas, 1971, p. 17. Stanley's article 'Absolution' appeared in *Nineteenth Century*, Jan. 1878.

[4] G. W. E. Russell, *Edward King*, pp. 161 n. and 146.

[5] Ibid., p. 147. Lockhart, *Viscount Halifax*, ii. 18. *Lincolnshire Chronicle*, 15 June 1888.

Two willing parishioners, John Marshall and Felix Thomas
Wilson, were eventually found, and William Brown, a solicitor
from Grimsby, helped to draw up the petition.

Benson at first said he had no jurisdiction to act, but when
the Privy Council disagreed he decided to put the Bishop on
on trial.[1] High Churchmen were horrified. Lord Halifax
bitterly criticized the Archbishop to the E.C.U. He 'loved pose
and effect', said G. W. E. Russell, and 'longed to assert his
jurisdiction'. Mackarness spoke of 'a Canterbury papacy'.
William Bright, Liddon, Paget, Charles Gore, and others all
urged King to protest. King's own objection was that to be
tried only by the metropolitan jeopardized the position of the
other bishops; the proper court was the Archbishop and other
provincial bishops in Convocation.[2]

The trial took place at Lambeth Palace. Some still doubted
its legality,[3] but the Archbishop considered the objections and
came to the same conclusion as the Privy Council, 'although',
he added, 'by an entirely different line of enquiry'.[4] Benson
appointed five assessors, Temple, Stubbs, Thorold, John
Wordsworth, and Atlay, none of whom, however, was to have a
part in the judgement itself. Wordsworth was an open opponent
of the Public Worship Regulation Act.[5] Stubbs agreed to serve
only under pressure from Dean Church, and told everyone, 'It
is not a Court; it is an Archbishop sitting in his library.'[6] The
bishops wore scarlet; King wore a fur-lined coat given to him
by the historian H. O. Wakeman, as if to emphasize his
detachment from what was going on. Liddon, who was a
confirmed misogynist, added that 'the great ecclesiastical
ladies, who flit about in the surrounding atmosphere, add an
element of grotesqueness to the whole thing.'[7]

Notwithstanding the misgivings of High Churchmen,
Benson's sympathies lay entirely with King. 'Anything', he

[1] *Ex parte Read*, 13 P.D. 221.
[2] Lockhart, op. cit. ii. 21 f. G. W. E. Russell, op. cit., pp. 149 and 163. *Letters of William Stubbs*, ed. W. H. Hutton, 1904, p. 322.
[3] *The Times*, 12 Feb. 1889, p. 10.
[4] *The Bishop of Lincoln's Case*, ed. E. S. Roscoe, 1891, p. 42.
[5] Watson, *The Life of Bishop John Wordsworth*, p. 99. He also opposed the notion that Benson could try King sitting alone: pp. 249 ff.
[6] Hutton, op. cit., p. 327. B. A. Smith, *Dean Church*, pp. 200 f.
[7] Letter of 14 Feb. 1889, quoted by G. W. E. Russell, op. cit., p. 167. For Liddon on women, see H. S. Holland, *Personal Studies*, n. d., p. 164.

said, 'can be forgiven to this Bishop, so sweet and so manly.' On the day of King's alleged offences he too had preached at St. Peter-at-Gowts, observing only that the 'good Vicar, Townsend', had been one of his pupils, and that in the morning King had not produced his mitre.[1] His judgement upheld the Bishop in almost every respect, criticizing only the sign of the cross ('an innovation, which must be discontinued') and the concealment of the manual acts during the consecration, about which the Bishop had 'mistaken the true order of the Holy Communion'. The Archbishop added that the commixture ought to take place (if at all) before the service began.[2] Sir Horace Davey asked for costs on behalf of the prosecutors; none were given. King, who was not present when the judgement was delivered, received a telegram from his counsel, Sir Walter Phillimore (Chancellor of Lincoln and a vice-president of the E.C.U.): *Mistio in media celebratione signum crucis prohibita. Populus debet videre actus manuales. Omnia alia pro te. In necessariis victoria.*[3] The Archbishop, said Phillimore, 'has given you all the important things, and he has reduced (as it seems to me) those things which he has not given you to even less importance.'[4]

King told his diocese that he still thought trial by synod would have been better; but he instantly obeyed the judgement, pointing out that his ritual was not obligatory on anyone else.[5] He wanted now to 'teach the people that we are not lawless, or Romish, but loyal English Catholics'.[6] In fact the trial had completely discredited his detractors. Moderate Evangelicals counselled the complainants not to appeal against the judgement to the Privy Council, but the extremists disagreed.[7] Read appealed, and the Judicial Committee upheld Benson's judgement. During the affair every ruri-decanal conference in the diocese had voted its confidence in the Bishop. A defence fund of £2,750 was subscribed within a month. 'Oh! how blessed a thing it is to have been allowed to love you,' wrote

---

[1] A. C. Benson, *The Life of E. W. Benson*, 1898, ii. 151 and 152.

[2] Roscoe (ed.), op. cit., pp. 176 and 145.

[3] Lockhart, op. cit. ii. 23.

[4] Russell, op. cit., p. 183.

[5] *Lincoln Diocesan Magazine*, Jan. 1891, p. 200.

[6] Russell, op. cit., p. 210.

[7] Cf. *Church Times*, 12 Dec. 1890, and the letter by J. T. Tomlinson, *Guardian*, 5 June 1891.

Henry Scott Holland during the trial. Those who disliked King's ritualism none the less found the trial distasteful. Benson's daughter was 'astonished at a man so absolutely saintly making such a tremendous fuss over trifles'. If King did not think them trifles, she said, 'his views must be horribly materialistic', although she hoped that he would be acquitted. Even *The Times*, as Bright observed, was far more pacific than people had expected.[1]

High Churchmen were jubilant. The judgement, said Dean Church, was 'the most courageous thing that has come from Lambeth for the last two hundred years'. Benson had changed the whole basis of the whole controversy; he completely ignored the judgements of the Privy Council in previous ritual cases, and, as his daughter observed, he took pleasure in continually correcting and lecturing the lawyers.[2] Instead he appealed to history, citing twenty-three authorities from the Council of Hatfield in A.D. 680, to *Lucy* v. *the Bishop of St. David's* in 1702, and referring in his judgement not only to Reformers like Cranmer and Tyndale, but also to Laud and Cosin, to Ambrose and Basil and Chrysostom, and to the Mozarabic and Clementine liturgies.[3] In rejecting Read's appeal to the Privy Council, the Lord Chancellor, Halsbury, drew attention to the importance of this historical evidence.[4] By appealing to what was thought to be antiquity, the judgement recognized, said the *Guardian*, 'that the Church of England of the present is historically one with the Church of England of the past; that . . . she was not the creation of Henry VIII or Edward VI.'[5] This was what High Churchmen and ritualists had always asserted. As Newman had written in 1837, 'Catholicity, Apostolicity, and consent of the Fathers, is the proper evidence of the fidelity or apostolicity of a professed Tradition.'[6]

[1] Russell, op. cit., pp. 156, 168, 179, and 197. A. C. Benson, *Life and Letters of Maggie Benson*, 1917, pp. 112 f.

[2] M. C. Church, op. cit., p. 349. Benson, *Maggie Benson*, p. 112.

[3] Roscoe (ed.), op. cit., pp. 54–90 and 101 ff.

[4] *Read* v. *Bishop of Lincoln*, L.R. Appeal Cases 1892.

[5] *Guardian*, 26 Nov. 1890.

[6] J. H. Newman, *Lectures on the Prophetical Office of the Church*, 1837, p. 62.

VI

CONCLUSION

THE first four ritualist imprisonments so effectively discredited the Public Worship Regulation Act that historians
have tended to forget Bell Cox.[1] Tait confessed to Disraeli
on 1 February 1881 'that the Act of 1874 has not worked
smoothly'.[2] The Lincoln judgement thwarted attempts to find
new ways of prosecution. In spite of the initial doubts enter-
tained by High Churchmen, Scott Holland admitted that
Benson's action 'saved the day', 'saved the position', 'broke up
prosecutions', and 'shattered the reputation of the Privy
Council'.[3] The Evangelical Edward Bickersteth, who was
consecrated Bishop of Exeter in 1885, said that he hoped the
Rector of Tedburn St. Mary would obey his monition to give
up using wafer bread, candles, and vestments, but he added that,
in the present state of the law, prosecutions on such matters
'only aggravate the evils they are intended to suppress'. The
Bishop of London, Mandell Creighton, said that 'Prosecutions
were abandoned, because it was found that they absolutely
failed'. Between 1874 and 1906 the bishops vetoed thirty-three
attempts to prosecute.[4]

In 1880 Justin McCarthy observed that on the whole the
Public Worship Regulation Act had 'promoted rather than
suppressed Ritualism'. The victimization of Edward King
seven years later served only to heighten sympathy for the
ritualists. By 1898, according to Hensley Henson, one clergyman
in six was a High Churchman (and one layman in twenty).

[1] S. Low and L. C. Sanders, *The Political History of England*, vol. xii, 1913, p. 274;
W. H. Hutton in *Social England*, ed. H. D. Traill and J. S. Mann, 1904, ix. 591.
W. B. Carpenter, *History of the Church of England*, 1919, p. 470, and E. W. Stratford,
The Victorian Sunset, 1931, p. 131, manage to reduce the number imprisoned to
two or three!
[2] Beaconsfield Papers, B/XII/F19.
[3] Holland, *Personal Studies*, p. 117.
[4] *The Protestant Dictionary*, ed. C. S. Clarke and G. E. A. Weeks, 1933, p. 554.
Memoirs of Archbishop Temple, ed. Sandford, ii. 103. G. K. A. Bell, *Randall Davidson*,
i. 533 n.

In 1904 it was said that any new court set up to deal with the growth of the ritualistic conspiracy would require the institution of some 4,000 or 5,000 separate suits.[1]

Not that King's trial ended controversy: Harcourt remained actively hostile; Randall Davidson (who had wanted Bell Cox to submit to Ryle, and who, during the trial of Bishop King, asserted that the matter could be 'quickly and quietly solved' if men would only have the sense to agree on a court of un-challenged jurisdiction) became Bishop of Winchester and in 1895 managed to force the Revd. R. R. Dolling to resign from St. Agatha's, Landport, because of his ritualist practices. These seasoned combatants were supported by men who had been too young to prosecute ritualists earlier. Winston Churchill, for instance, who was born in 1874, pencilled against the account of the passing of the Public Worship Regulation Act in his copy of the *Annual Register* the comment that 'If a Church is "established" and receives recognition from the Government ... it is obvious that the Government should be able to insist on effective control.' In 1899, standing as a Tory Democrat in Oldham, he announced that if the ecclesiastical machinery for dealing with lawlessness in the Church had broken down, it ought to be speedily repaired or replaced, and 'if the authority of the bishops is not exerted or obeyed, stronger measures will be necessary'.[2] Between that year and 1902, six bills against ritualism were introduced in the House of Commons. All failed; but as a result of the agitation Balfour was forced to set up a Royal Commission on Ecclesiastical Discipline.[3]

The fourteen members of the commission, representing most shades of current Anglican opinion, sat 118 times between 1904 and 1906 and examined 164 witnesses. Their conclusions were that 'the machinery for discipline has broken down', and that the Public Worship Regulation Act should be repealed. As the Bishop of Chester said in his evidence, it was 'notorious' that as soon as the act began to operate, 'the very people who had

[1] McCarthy, *A History of Our Own Times*, iv. 417. H. H. Henson, *Cui Bono: an Open Letter to Lord Halifax*, 1898, p. 29. Eccles. Discipline *Report*, 5638; cf. the statistics at 4581.

[2] Bell, op. cit. i. 137, 263 ff., 339. R. S. Churchill, *Winston S. Churchill*, vol. i, 1966, pp. 335 and 445.

[3] Eccles. Discipline *Report*, 7397, 1216, and p. 63 paras. 350, 351; Bell, op. cit., pp. 459 f.

clamoured for that legislation began to see its grave defects'.[1]

In spite of the ritualists' opponents, the 1874 Act had been defeated. The Church of England had changed; indeed, four of those who had voted against the act, Gladstone, Salisbury, Balfour, and Campbell-Bannerman, subsequently became prime ministers, and preferred to the episcopal bench men whose ritualist leanings would have horrified Tait. It is possible to view the whole controversy as a 'futile battle', an affair of 'petty excitements';[2] but the truth is that it involved far-reaching consequences for the Church.

It inaugurated the liturgical agonizing which characterized the Church of England in the twentieth century. The most important concession to the ritualists made by the Royal Commission in 1906 was the statement that 'The law of public worship in the Church of England is too narrow for the religious life of the present generation', since it was laid down when men did not fully appreciate ceremonial or dignity and lacked a sense of the continuity of the Church.[3] It had become clear that the demands of worship had outgrown the rubrics, and the commission recommended that new ones be enacted. Almost immediately it was realized that this was not enough: the Church of England needed an entirely revised Prayer Book.[4] One of the concerns of the first Tractarians had been to prevent a parliament no longer composed entirely of Anglicans from tampering with the Prayer Book;[5] their ritualist successors were concerned to persuade a similarly constructed parliament that the Prayer Book was not good enough. But the passions roused by the controversy ensured that not until the primacy of Arthur Michael Ramsey, Archbishop of Canterbury from 1961 to 1974, did the Church gain freedom from Parliament to order and revise its own forms of worship.[6]

The commissioners in 1906 clearly took at face value the ritualists' claim that their practices derived from the early

---

[1] Eccles. Discipline *Report*, 14480; p. 70, para. 380; and p. 76, para. 400.

[2] D. L. Edwards, *Leaders of the Church of England, 1828–1944*, 1971, p. 119.

[3] Eccles. Discipline *Report*, pp. 75–6, para. 399.

[4] *Walter Howard Frere: His Correspondence on Liturgical Revision and Construction*, ed. R. C. D. Jasper, 1954, pp. 4 ff.

[5] L. F. Barmann, 'The Liturgical Dimension of the Oxford Tracts', *Journal of British Studies*, 1968, pp. 92–113.

[6] A. M. Ramsay, *Whose Hearts God has Touched*, 1961, pp. 5 f.

Church.[1] This claim was largely spurious: altar crosses and candles, for instance, far from being sanctioned by Saint Justin Martyr and the Old Testament respectively, had been regarded (as Edmund Bishop put it) with 'a certain chariness' as late as the thirteenth century.[2] Edmund Bishop was the outstanding liturgical scholar of the time, and his conception of the simplicity, sobriety, and self-control of the Roman mass[3] made him pour scorn on most ritualist notions. He told a French Roman Catholic in 1895 that young people entering the ritualist movement at that time 'actually believe that the Church of England was always like that, and they will not believe anything else'.[4]

In fact, in spite of—even because of—their antiquarianism and Roman borrowings, the ethos of the ritualists was essentially romantic and Victorian. 'Mystery', wrote Edmund Bishop, 'never flourished in the Roman atmosphere, and symbolism was no product of the Roman religious mind.'[5] But mystery and symbolism were precisely what the ritualists sought. They would have agreed with an announcement made by Oakeley in 1840—'We are for carrying out the symbolical principle in our own Church'—had Oakeley not added the duty of obedience to the rubrics.[6]

This was a new element in Anglicanism. As Fr. Lowder wrote, the ritualists (partly by the example of what he described as 'the daily sacrifice of their lives') taught that ritual was 'not a mere aesthetic embellishment, but the outward expression of a great reality', namely their Lord's sacramental Presence.[7] The poem written by Mrs. Hamilton King on the death of Mackonochie is a literary expression of the ritualists' powerfully

---

[1] e.g. Edward King to the Revd. E. T. Gibbons in 1874, in Russell, *Edward King*, p. 46.

[2] Compare B. Street, *In Search of Ritual*, 1867, p. 26, and T. P. Dale, *The S. Vedast Case*, 1881, pp. 5–6, with E. Bishop 'The Christian Altar', in *Liturgica Historica*, 1918, p. 28.

[3] E. Bishop, 'The Genius of the Roman Rite' (1899), in *Liturgica Historica*, 1918, p. 12.

[4] N. Abercrombie, *The Life and Work of Edmund Bishop*, 1959, p. 226.

[5] Ibid., p. 10.

[6] F. Oakeley in *British Critic*, Jan.–Apr. 1840, p. 270, quoted O. Chadwick, *The Mind of the Oxford Movement*, 1960, p. 56.

[7] C. F. Lowder, *Twenty-One Years in St. George's Mission*, 1877, pp. 163 f.

romantic notion that earthly worship could and should directly represent worship at the heavenly altar:

> Oh, awful is the wilderness,
>   And pitiless the snow;
> But down in dim St. Alban's
>   The seven lamps burn aglow,
> And softly in the Sanctuary
>   The priest moves to and fro,
> And with one heart the people pray;
>   And this is home below.
>
> And higher, in the House of God,
>   Seven lamps before the Throne,
> The golden vials of odours sweet,
>   The voice of praise alone;
> With the beloved, the redeemed,
>   Whose toil and tears are done,—
> And this is in the Father's Home
>   That waits for every one.[1]

Such a ready access to the heavenly altar, in a fashion denied to their opponents, led the ritualists to some occasional arrogance; they found it easy to denigrate others. Liddon explained to Lady Salisbury that the Archbishop of Canterbury was 'apparently ignorant or distrustful of the resources of any spiritual or moral power whatever'.[2] When A. P. Stanley died, Dean Church wrote that amongst his defects was an 'incapacity for the spiritual and unearthly side of religion; the side which is so strong in the people whom he opposed, Newman and Keble, and, in a lower way, the Evangelicals; the elevations and aspiration after Divine affections, and longings after God . . .'[3] When Edward King was preferred to Lincoln, on the other hand, Church described him as 'an improved type of the S. François de Sales kind, a type much wanting in the English Church'.[4] Such a stance was perhaps necessary to maintain the high morale of a persecuted group.

[1] E. A. T., *A. H. Mackonochie*, ed. E. F. Russell, p. 329, quoting from Mrs. King's *Ballads of the North*.

[2] Salisbury Papers, class H: Special Correspondence, Liddon to Lady Salisbury, 21 Apr. 1874.

[3] M. C. Church, *Dean Church*, p. 293.

[4] Gladstone Papers, Additional MS. 44127, R. W. Church to Gladstone, 2 Feb. 1885.

Their persecution marked a further stage in a crucial and unsolved issue: that of authority in the Church of England. *Vanity Fair* observed of Archbishop Tait that he displayed 'a power, rarely found in a priest, of treating public affairs from a statesman's point of view'.[1] He treated church affairs from the same point of view, and in doing so brought to the boil a pot that had simmered since the Gorham case. The relationship between the issues of sacramentalism and authority in the ritualist controversy is well brought out in the exchange of letters between Liddon and Gladstone after the Purchas judgement: Liddon asserted initially that in attacking the eastward position the decision went 'the whole length of proscribing any adequate expression of Sacramental belief in the ritual of the Church of England'; he added that the position was used by many 'old fashioned and well educated high churchmen' and that the judgement 'would have condemned Mr. Keble, had he been still among us'. Gladstone replied that the restrictions laid upon Christians by the judgement were scarcely capable of being rated higher than a hardship, 'to be borne, in this world, like many other hardships', whereupon Liddon immediately changed his ground and countered that the constitution of the court was the real point at issue.[2]

Others came to see that no court, however constituted, could deal with such problems. The failure of the Public Worship Regulation Act taught responsible churchmen and parliamentarians that men like Bishop Mackarness of Oxford had been wise in thinking there must be some 'more excellent way' of settling religious disputes than by process of law.[3] In 1878 Bishop T. L. Claughton conceded that 'The operation of the Act has been the reverse of what was expected'; he now believed that legal methods provided no remedy for ritualist disorders.[4] Unfortunately the controversy produced no other remedy.

Most ritualists remained aggressively obdurate. 'Not all the parliaments in the world,' Archdeacon Denison preached, 'nor

---

[1] *Vanity Fair*, 25 Dec. 1869, p. 361.

[2] Gladstone Papers, Additional MS. 44237, Liddon to Gladstone, 25 Feb. 1871; Gladstone to Liddon, 26 Feb. 1871; Liddon's reply, 28 Feb. 1871.

[3] Gladstone Papers, Additional MS. 44444, Mackarness to Gladstone, 2 Aug. 1874.

[4] T. L. Claughton, *A Charge delivered to the Clergy and Churchwardens of the Diocese of St. Alban's*, 1878, p. 32.

all the Courts in the world can "put down Ritualism". They may persecute and imprison and ruin Priests here and there. They may damage irreparably Congregations of faithful men; but one thing they cannot do, and that is "put down Ritualism".' As he correctly observed, to attempt to do so was like trying to put down the doctrine of the Real Presence,[1] as if one man could alter the beliefs of another by law. Tait, said Canon Gregory of St. Paul's, was setting up a new Star Chamber in 1874 to stop men celebrating facing east—thereby destroying 'a right enjoyed by English Churchmen since the Reformation'.[2] In truth, the new Star Chamber, if it was one, was set up not by Tait but by Parliament—a fact which, as we have seen, had important consequences for the relationship between Church and State.

Less pugnacious High Churchmen perceived that the 1874 Act raised a central Victorian issue, that of individual liberty. In a letter thanking Lord Salisbury for attacking the bill, one clergyman wrote, 'All we want and believe as Englishmen we shall not seek in vain is Toleration.'[3] Tait himself had tried to win Salisbury to his point of view by arguing that 'the discretion of the individual incumbent ought to be subject to control'.[4] But his method was too savage, especially for the professional and gentlemanly classes. William Stubbs, the exceptionally intelligent High Churchman who had been made Regius professor of modern history at Oxford, set down his objections to the whole enterprise in June 1874. Writing, he said, as one who was no ritualist but who had worked for many years as a parish priest, he believed that the bill constituted a 'fatal blow that threatens the moral and spiritual as well as the temporal status of the clergy. A change in the tenure of church preferment, such as is now proposed, must not only repel candidates for Holy Orders, must not only prevent men of independent thought and learning from undertaking such a humiliating position, but must seem to destroy the legal position of those who accepted preferment under other and fairer conditions.'

[1] Denison, *A Charge of the Archdeacon . . . April 1877*, p. 14.
[2] Salisbury Papers, Class H, Special Correspondence, Gregory to Salisbury, 10 Mar. 1874.
[3] Ibid., M/74/05/10.
[4] Ibid., Class H, Special Correspondence, Tait to Salisbury, 18 Mar. 1874.

If Tait's plans were not destroyed, he concluded, the parish priest would be 'at the mercy of the beershopkeeper'.[1]

Tait's plans were, however, eventually destroyed, and those of Parliament too. As another Oxford professor, Dr. Sanday, told the Royal Commission on Ecclesiastical Discipline thirty years later, it had become clear that where there seemed to be a collision between the Church and the civil power, men would go to prison rather than submit. That they were prepared to defy the State in this way showed, he believed, how far the Oxford Movement had affected the Church of England over the course of seventy years. And in the face of such defiance others were coming to terms with beliefs which they had previously found intolerable. It was Sanday's hope that 'Distinct Churches and distinct parties will not cease to exist, but they will learn to tolerate and respect each other.'[2] By refusing to be put down, the ritualists not only preserved the Anglican clergyman's ancient freedom; they also advanced the cause of toleration in Victorian Britain.

[1] Salisbury Papers, Class H, Special Correspondence, Stubbs to Salisbury, 20 June, 1874.
[2] Eccles. Discipline *Report*, 16362 and 16379; cf. 16410. Sanday was Lady Margaret professor of divinity.

APPENDIX

AN ACT for the better administration of the Laws respecting the Regulation of Public Worship. (7th August 1874)

(Preamble.)

1. This Act may be cited as 'The Public Worship Regulation Act, 1874.' — Short title.

3.* This Act shall extend to that part of the United Kingdom called England, to the Channel Islands, and the Isle of Man. — Extent of Act.

4. Proceedings taken under this Act shall not be deemed to be such proceedings as are mentioned in the Church Discipline Act, 1840, section twenty-three. — Proceedings under this Act not to be deemed proceedings under 3 & 4 Vict. c. 86. s. 23.

5. Nothing in this Act contained, save as herein expressly provided, shall be construed to affect or repeal any jurisdiction which may now be in force for the due administration of ecclesiastical law. — Savings of Jurisdiction.

6. In this Act the following terms shall, if not inconsistent with the context, be thus interpreted— — Interpretation of terms.

The term 'bishop' means the archbishop or bishop of the diocese in which the church or burial ground is situate to which a representation relates: — 'Bishop.'

The term 'Book of Common Prayer' means the book annexed to the Act of the fourteenth year of the reign of King Charles the Second, chapter four, intituled 'The Book of Common Prayer, and administration of the Sacraments, and other Rites and Ceremonies of the — 'Book of Common Prayer.'

* S. 2 rep. 56 & 57 Vict. c. 54 (S.L.R.).

Church, according to the use of the Church of England; together with the Psalter or Psalms of David, pointed as they are to be sung or said in churches; and the form or manner of making, ordaining, and consecrating of Bishops, Priests, and Deacons'; together with such alterations as have from time to time been or may hereafter be made in the said book by lawful authority:

The term 'burial ground' means any churchyard, cemetery, or burial ground, or the part of any cemetery or burial ground, in which, at the burial of any corpse therein, the order for the burial of the dead contained in the Book of Common Prayer is directed by law to be used: | 'Burial ground.'

The term 'church' means any church, chapel, or place of public worship in which the incumbent is by law or by the terms of license from the bishop required to conduct divine service according to the Book of Common Prayer: | 'Church.'

The term 'diocese' means the diocese in which the church or burial ground is situate to which a representation relates, and comprehends all places which are situate within the limits of such diocese: | 'Diocese.'

The term 'incumbent' means the person or persons in holy orders legally responsible for the due performance of divine service in any church, or of the order for the burial of the dead in any burial ground: | 'Incumbent.'

The term 'parish' means any parish, ecclesiastical district, chapelry, or place, over which any incumbent has the exclusive cure of souls: | 'Parish.'

The term 'parishioner' means a male person of full age who before making any representation under this Act has transmitted to the bishop under his hand the declaration contained in Schedule (A.) to this Act, and who has, and for one year next before taking any proceeding under this Act has had, his usual place of abode in the parish within which the church or burial ground is situate, or for the use of which the burial ground is legally provided, to which the representation relates: *'Parishioner.'*

The term 'barrister-at-law' shall in the Isle of Man include advocate: *'Barrister-at-law.'*

The term 'rules and orders' means the rules and orders framed under the provisions of this Act. *'Rules and orders.'*

7. The Archbishop of Canterbury and the Archbishop of York may, but subject to the approval of Her Majesty to be signified under Her Sign Manual, appoint from time to time a barrister-at-law who has been in actual practice for ten years, or a person who has been a judge of one of the Superior Courts of Law or Equity, or of any court, to which the jurisdiction of any such court has been or may hereafter be transferred by authority of Parliament, to be, during good behaviour, a judge of the Provincial Courts of Canterbury and York, herein-after called the judge. *Appointment and duties of judge.*

If the said archbishop shall not, within six months after the occurrence of any vacancy in the office, appoint the said judge, Her Majesty may by Letters Patent appoint some person qualified as aforesaid, to be such judge.

Whensoever a vacancy shall occur in the office of official principal of the Arches Court of Canterbury, the judge shall

become ex officio such official principal,
and all proceedings thereafter taken before
the judge in relation to matters arising
within the province of Canterbury shall
be deemed to be taken in the Arches
Court of Canterbury; and whensoever a
vacancy shall occur in the office of official principal or auditor of the Chancery
Court of York, the judge shall become ex
officio such official principal or auditor,
and all proceedings thereafter taken
before the judge in relation to matters
arising within the province of York shall
be deemed to be taken in the Chancery
Court of York; and whensoever a vacancy
shall occur in the office of Master of the
Faculties to the Archbishop of Canterbury, such judge shall become ex officio
such Master of the Faculties.

Every person appointed to be a judge under
this Act shall be a member of the Church
of England, and shall, before entering
on his office, sign the declaration in
Schedule (A.) to this Act; and if at any
time any such judge shall cease to be a
member of the Church, his office shall
thereupon be vacant.

8. If the archdeacon of the archdeaconry or a
churchwarden of the parish, or any three
parishioners of the parish, within which
archdeaconry or parish any church or
burial ground is situate, or for the use of
any part of which any burial ground is
legally provided, or in case of cathedral or
collegiate churches, any three inhabitants
of the diocese, being male persons of full
age, who have signed and transmitted to
the bishop under their hands the declaration contained in Schedule (A.) under
this Act, and who have, and for one year
next before taking any proceeding under
this Act have had, their usual place of
abode in the diocese within which the

Representation by archdeacon, churchwarden, parishioners or inhabitants of diocese.

cathedral or collegiate church is situated,
shall be of opinion,—

(1) That in such church any alteration in
or addition to the fabric, ornaments,
or furniture thereof has been made
without lawful authority, or that any
decoration forbidden by law has been
introduced into such church; or

(2) That the incumbent has within the
preceding twelve months used or
permitted to be used in such church
or burial ground any unlawful ornament of the minister of the church, or
neglected to use any prescribed ornament or vesture; or

(3) That the incumbent has within the
preceding twelve months failed to
observe, or to cause to be observed,
the directions contained in the Book
of Common Prayer relating to the
performance, in such church or burial
ground, of the services, rites, and
ceremonies ordered by the said book,
or has made or permitted to be made
any unlawful addition to, alteration
of, or omission from, such services,
rites, and ceremonies,—

such archdeacon, churchwarden, parishioners, or such inhabitants of the diocese,
may, if he or they think fit, represent the
same to the bishop, by sending to the
bishop a form, as contained in Schedule
(B) to this Act, duly filled up and signed,
and accompanied by a declaration made
by him or them under the Statutory
Declarations Act, 1835, affirming the
truth of the statements contained in the
representation: Provided, that no proceedings shall be taken under this Act as
regards any alteration in or addition to the
fabric of a church if such alteration or
addition has been completed five years

5 & 6 Will. 4.
c. 62.

before the commencement of such proceedings.

9. Unless the bishop shall be of opinion, after
considering the whole circumstances of
the case, that proceedings should not be
taken on the representation, (in which
case he shall state in writing the reason for
his opinion, and such statement shall be
deposited in the registry of the diocese,
and a copy thereof shall forthwith be
transmitted to the person or some one of
the persons who shall have made the
representation, and to the person complained of,) he shall within twenty-one
days after receiving the representation
transmit a copy thereof to the person
complained of, and shall require such
person, and also the person making the
representation, to state in writing within
twenty-one days whether they are willing
to submit to the directions of the bishop
touching the matter of the said representation, without appeal; and, if they
shall state their willingness to submit
to the directions of the bishop without
appeal, the bishop shall forthwith proceed
to hear the matter of the representation
in such manner as he shall think fit, and
shall pronounce such judgment and issue
such monition (if any) as he may think
proper, and no appeal shall lie from such
judgment or monition.

*Proceedings on
representation.*

Provided, that no judgment so pronounced
by the bishop shall be considered as
finally deciding any questions of law so
that it may not be again raised by other
parties.

The parties may, at any time after the
making of a representation to the bishop,
join in stating any questions arising in
such proceedings in a special case signed
by a barrister-at-law for the opinion of the

judge, and the parties after signing and transmitting the same to the bishop may require it to be transmitted to the judge for hearing, and the judge shall hear and determine the question or questions arising thereon, and any judgment pronounced by the bishop shall be in conformity with such determination.

If the person making the representation and the person complained of shall not, within the time aforesaid, state their willingness to submit to the directions of the bishop, the bishop shall forthwith transmit the representation in the mode prescribed by the rules and orders to the archbishop of the province, and the archbishop shall forthwith require the judge to hear the matter of the representation at any place within the diocese or province, or in London or Westminster.

The judge shall give not less than twenty-eight days notice to the parties of the time and place at which he will proceed to hear the matter of the said representation. The judge before proceeding to give such notice shall require from the person making the representation such security for costs as the judge may think proper, such security to be given in the manner prescribed by the rules and orders.

The person complained of shall within twenty-one days after such notice transmit to the judge, and to the person making the representation, a succinct answer to the representation, and in default of such answer he shall be deemed to have denied the truth or relevancy of the representation.

In all proceedings before the judge under this Act the evidence shall be given viva voce, in open court, and upon oath: and the judge shall have the powers of a court of record, and may require and enforce the attendance of witnesses, and the production of evidences, books, or writings, in the like manner as a judge of one of the superior courts of law or equity, or of any court to which the jurisdiction of any such court has been or may hereafter be transferred by authority of Parliament.

Unless the parties shall both agree that the evidence shall be taken down by a shorthand writer, and that a special case shall not be stated, the judge shall state the facts proved before him in the form of a special case, similar to a special case stated under the Common Law Procedure Acts, 1852–1854.

15 & 16 Vict. c. 76. 17 & 18 Vict. c. 125.

The judge shall pronounce judgment on the matter of the representation, and shall deliver to the parties, on application, and to the bishop, a copy of the special case, if any, and judgment.

The judge shall issue such monition (if any) and make such order as to costs as the judgment shall require.

The judge may, on application in any case, suspend the execution of such monition pending an appeal, if he shall think fit.

10. The registrar of the diocese, or his deputy duly appointed shall perform such duties in relation to this Act and shall receive such fees as may be prescribed by the rules and orders.

Registrar of the diocese to perform duties under the Act.

11. In any proceedings under this Act either party may appear either by himself in person or by counsel, or by any proctor or any attorney or solicitor.

Parties may appear in person or by counsel, &c.

12. For the purpose of an appeal to Her Majesty in Council under this Act, the special case settled by the judge, or a copy of the shorthand writer's notes, as the case may

No fresh evidence to be admitted on appeal.

be, shall be transmitted in the manner prescribed by rules and orders, and no fresh evidence shall be admitted upon appeal except by the permission of the tribunal hearing the appeal.

13. Obedience by an incumbent to a monition or order of the bishop or judge, as the case may be, shall be enforced, if necessary, in the manner prescribed by rules and orders, by an order inhibiting the incumbent from performing any service of the church, or otherwise exercising the cure of souls within the diocese for a term not exceeding three months; provided that at the expiration of such term the inhibition shall not be relaxed until the incumbent shall, by writing under his hand, in the form prescribed by the rules and orders, undertake to pay due obedience to such monition or order, or to the part thereof which shall not have been annulled: Provided that if such inhibition shall remain in force for more than three years from the date of the issuing of the monition, or from the final determination of an appeal therefrom, whichever shall last happen, or if a second inhibition in regard to the same monition shall be issued within three years from the relaxation of an inhibition, any benefice or other ecclesiastical preferment held by the incumbent in the parish in which the church or burial ground is situate, or for the use of which the burial ground is legally provided, in relation to which church or burial ground such monition has been issued as aforesaid, shall thereupon become void, unless the bishop shall, for some special reason stated by him in writing postpone for a period not exceeding three months the date at which, unless such inhibition be relaxed, such benefice or other ecclesias-

Inhibition of incumbent.

tical preferment shall become void as aforesaid; and upon any such avoidance it shall be lawful for the patron of such benefice or other ecclesiastical preferment to appoint, present, collate, or nominate to the same as if such incumbent were dead; and the provisions contained in the Pluralities Act, 1838, section fifty-eight, in reference to notice to the patron and as to lapse, shall be applicable to any benefice or other ecclesiastical preferment avoided under this Act; and it shall not be lawful for the patron at any time to appoint, present, collate, or nominate to such benefice or such other ecclesiastical preferment the incumbent by whom the same was avoided under this Act. *1 & 2 Vict. c. 106, s. 58.*

The bishop may, during such inhibition, unless he is satisfied that due provision is otherwise made for the spiritual charge of the parish, make due provision for the service of the church and the cure of souls, and it shall be lawful for the bishop to raise the sum required from time to time for such provision by sequestration of the profits of such benefice or other ecclesiastical preferment.

Any question as to whether a monition or order given or issued after proceedings before the bishop or judge, as the case may be, has or has not been obeyed shall be determined by the bishop or the judge, and any proceedings to enforce obedience to such monition or order shall be taken by direction of the judge.

14. It shall not be necessary to obtain a faculty from the ordinary in order lawfully to obey any monition issued under this Act, and if the judge shall direct in any monition that a faculty shall be applied for, such fees only shall be paid for such faculty as may be directed by the rules and orders: *Faculty not necessary in certain cases.*

Provided that nothing in this Act contained shall be construed to limit or control the discretion vested by law in the ordinary as to the grant or refusal of a faculty: Provided also, that a faculty shall, on application, be granted, if unopposed, on payment of such a fee (not exceeding two guineas) as shall be prescribed by the rules and orders, in respect of any alteration in or addition to the fabric of any church, or in respect of any ornaments or furniture, not being contrary to law, made or existing in any church at the time of the passing of this Act.

15. All notices and other documents directed to be given to any person under this Act shall be given in the manner prescribed by rules and orders.

Service of notices.

16. If any bishop shall be patron of the benefice or of any ecclesiastical preferment held by the incumbent respecting whom a representation shall have been made, or shall be unable from illness to discharge any of the duties imposed upon him by this Act in regard to any representation, the archbishop of the province shall act in the place of such bishop in all matters thereafter arising in relation to such representation; and if any archbishop shall be patron of the benefice or of any ecclesiastical preferment held by the incumbent respecting whom a representation shall have been made, or shall be unable from illness to discharge any of the duties imposed upon him by this Act in regard to any representation, Her Majesty may, by Her Sign Manual, appoint an archbishop or bishop to act in the place of such archbishop in all matters thereafter arising in relation to such representation.

Substitute for bishop when patron, or in case of illness.

17. The duties appointed under this Act to be performed by the bishop of the diocese shall in the case of a cathedral or collegiate church be performed by the visitor thereof.

Provisions relating to cathedral or collegiate church.

If any complaint shall be made concerning the fabric, ornaments, furniture, or decorations of a cathedral or collegiate church, the person complained of shall be the dean and chapter of such cathedral or collegiate church, and in the event of obedience not being rendered to a monition relating to the fabric, ornaments, furniture, or decorations of such cathedral or collegiate church, the visitor, or the judge, as the case may be, shall have power to carry into effect the directions contained in such monition, and, if necessary, to raise the sum required to defray the cost thereof by sequestration of the profits of the preferments held in such cathedral or collegiate church by the dean and chapter thereof.

If any complaint shall be made concerning the ornaments of the minister in a cathedral or collegiate church, or as to the observance therein of the directions contained in the Book of Common Prayer, relating to the performance of the services, rites, and ceremonies ordered by the said book, or as to any alleged addition, to, alteration of, or omission from such services, rites, and ceremonies in such cathedral or collegiate church, the person complained of shall be the clerk in holy orders alleged to have offended in the matter complained of; and the visitor or the judge, as the case may be, in the event of obedience not being rendered to a monition, shall have the same power as to inhibition, and the preferment held in such cathedral or collegiate church by the person complained of shall be subject to the same conditions as to avoidance,

notice, and lapse, and as to any subsequent
appointment, presentation, collation, or
nomination thereto, and as to due provision being made for the performance of
the duties of such person, as are contained
in this Act concerning an incumbent to
whom a monition has been issued, and
concerning any benefice or other ecclesiastical preferment held by such incumbent.

18. When a sentence has been pronounced by
consent, or any suit or proceeding has
been commenced against any incumbent
under the Church Discipline Act, 1840,
he shall not be liable to proceedings under
this Act in respect of the same matter;
and no incumbent proceeded against
under this Act shall be liable to proceedings under the Church Discipline Act,
1840, in respect of any matter upon which
judgment has been pronounced under
this Act.

Limitation of proceedings against incumbent. 3 & 4 Vict. c. 86.

19. Her Majesty may by Order in Council,
at any time by and with the advice of the
Lord High Chancellor, the Lord Chief
Justice of England, the judge to be appointed under this Act, and the archbishops and bishops who are members
of Her Majesty's Privy Council, or any
two of the said persons, one of them
being the Lord High Chancellor or the
Lord Chief Justice of England, cause
rules and orders to be made for regulating
the procedure and settling the fees to be
taken in proceedings under this Act, so
far as the same may not be expressly
regulated by this Act, and from time to
time alter or amend such rules and orders.
All rules and orders made in pursuance
of this section shall be laid before each
House of Parliament within forty days
after the same are made, if Parliament is

Rules for settling procedure and fees under this Act.

then sitting, or if not, within forty days after the then next meeting of Parliament; and if an address is presented to Her Majesty by either of the said Houses within the next subsequent forty days on which the House shall have sat praying that any such rules may be annulled, Her Majesty may thereupon by Order in Council annul the same, and the rules and orders so annulled shall thenceforth become void, without prejudice to the validity of any proceedings already taken under the same.

SCHEDULES referred to in the foregoing Act

SCHEDULE (A)   Sects. 6, 7, 8

I do hereby solemnly declare that I am a member of the Church of England as by law established.

Witness my hand this   day of

SCHEDULE (B)   Sect. 8

PUBLIC WORSHIP REGULATION ACT, 1874

To the Right Rev. Father in God, A., by Divine permission Lord Bishop of B.

I (We) C.D., Archdeacon of the archdeaconry of   , (or a churchwarden or three parishioners of the parish of E.,) in your Lordship's diocese, do hereby represent that (the person or persons complained of) has or have (state the matter to be represented; if more than one, then under separate heads).

Dated this   day of   18
                              (Signed) D.D.

BIBLIOGRAPHY

MS SOURCES

Bath Papers, Longleat House.
Beaconsfield Papers, Hughenden Manor.
Cairns Papers, Public Record Office.
Cross Papers, British Library.
Gladstone Papers, British Library.
Papers on the Eastern Question, Public Record Office.
Salisbury Papers, Hatfield House (formerly at Christ Church, Oxford).
Tait Papers, Lambeth Palace.

OFFICIAL RECORDS

Acts of the Convocations of Canterbury and York.
Chronicle of Convocation.
Church Assembly Reports.
Clifton v. *Ridsdale*, 1 P.D. 316, 2 P.D. 376.
Ex Parte Read, 13 P.D. 221.
Hansard's Parliamentary Debates.
Julius v. *the Bishop of Oxford*, L.R. 5.
Report of the Royal Commission on Ecclesiastical Courts, 1883.
Report of the Royal Commission on Ecclesiastical Discipline, 1906.
The Statutes Revised, 3rd edn., 1950.

NEWSPAPERS AND JOURNALS

Beehive.
Bolton Evening News.
Builder.
Church Association Monthly Intelligencer.
Church Times.
Contemporary Review.
Daily Courier.
Dundee Advertiser.
Eccles and Patricroft Journal.
Eddows's Shrewsbury Journal.
Edinburgh Review.
Fortnightly Review.
Guardian.
Lincoln Diocesan Magazine.

Lincolnshire Chronicle.
Liverpool Mercury.
Nineteenth Century.
Northern Echo.
Pall Mall Gazette.
Parish Magazine of St. Mary Magdalene, Taunton.
Punch.
Quarterly Review.
Record.
Salisbury and Winchester Journal.
Staffordshire Sentinel.
Stockport Advertiser.
Sunday Times.
The Times.
Western Gazette.
Vanity Fair.
York Herald.

UNPUBLISHED M.A. THESIS

SHEEN, H. E., 'The Oxford Movement in a Manchester Parish: The Miles Platting Case', Manchester, 1941.

ARTICLES PUBLISHED ANONYMOUSLY

(Ashwell, A. R.), 'The State of the Church', *Quarterly Review*, vol. 137, July 1874, pp. 246–82.
(Capes, J. M.), 'Sacerdotalism Ancient and Modern', *Quarterly Review*, vol. 136, Jan. 1874, pp. 103–33.
(Freemantle, W. H.), 'Convocation, Parliament, and the Prayer-Book', *Edinburgh Review*, vol. 140, Oct. 1874, pp. 427–61.
(Shaw, Benjamin), 'Private Confession in the Church of England', *Quarterly Review*, vol. 124, Jan. 1868, pp. 83–116.
(Stanley, A. P.), 'Ritualism', *Edinburgh Review*, vol. 125, Apr. 1867, pp. 439–69.
(Thomson, W.), 'The Ritual of the English Church', *Quarterly Review*, vol. 137, Oct. 1874, pp. 542–86.

OTHER ARTICLES

ARNSTEIN, W. L., ed. and trans., 'A German View of English Society' (J. J. Weber *Illustrierter London-Führer*, Leipzig, 1851), *Victorian Studies*, vol. xvi, no. 2, Dec. 1972, pp. 187–203.
BAHLMAN, D. W. R., 'The Queen, Mr Gladstone, and Church Patronage', *Victorian Studies*, vol. iii, no. 4, June 1960, pp. 349–80.

BARMANN, L. F., 'The Liturgical Dimension of the Oxford Tracts', *Journal of British Studies*, 1968, pp. 92–113.

BENTLEY, J., 'British and German High Churchmen in the Struggle against Hitler', *Journal of Ecclesiastical History*, vol. xxiii, no. 3, July 1972, pp. 233–49.

BISHOP, E., 'The Christian Altar', *Liturgica Historica*, 1918, pp. 20–38.

—— 'The Genius of the Roman Rite', *Liturgica Historica*, 1918, pp. 1–19.

CHAMBERS, J. C., 'Private Confession and Absolution', *The Church and the World 1867*, 2nd edn., 1868, ed. O. Shipley, pp. 196–231.

—— 'A Layman's View of Confession', *The Church and the World 1867*, 2nd edn., 1868, pp. 336–98.

CLARK, G. KITSON, 'The Romantic Element, 1830–1850', *Studies in Social History*, ed. J. H. Plumb, 1955, pp. 211–39.

COWIE, L., 'Exeter Hall', *History Today*, June 1968, pp. 390–7.

FRASER, P., 'The Growth of Ministerial Control in the Nineteenth-Century House of Commons', *English Historical Review*, vol. 75, no. ccxcvi, July 1960, pp. 444–63.

GLADSTONE, W. E., 'Ritualism and Ritual', *Contemporary Review*, vol. xxiv, Oct. 1874, pp. 663–81.

GRIFFIN, J. R., 'The Radical Phase of the Oxford Movement', *Journal of Ecclesiastical History*, vol. 27, no. 1, Jan. 1976, pp. 47–56.

HARRISON, F., 'The Conservative Reaction', *Fortnightly Review*, new ser., vol. xv, Mar. 1874, pp. 297–309.

HOUSE, H., 'The Quality of George Eliot's Unbelief', *Ideas and Beliefs of the Victorians*, 1949, pp. 157–63.

JASPER, R. C. D., 'The Prayer Book in the Victorian Era', *The Victorian Crisis of Faith*, ed. A. Symondson, 1970, pp. 107–21.

McCORMACK, A., 'Cardinal Vaughan—The Fourth Cardinal', *Dublin Review*, no. 506, Winter 1965, pp. 295–336.

MAJOR, H. D. A., 'In Memorian Charles Gore', *Modern Churchman*, vol. xxi, Feb. 1932, pp. 581–3.

NEWMAN, F. W., 'Organized Priesthood', *Fortnightly Review*, new ser., vol. xv, Feb. 1874, pp. 176–89.

QUINAULT, R. E., 'The Fourth Party and the Religious Opposition to Bradlaugh', *English Historical Review*, vol. xci, no. 359, Apr. 1976, pp. 315–40.

ROBERTS, D. A., 'The Orange Order in Ireland: a religious institution', *British Journal of Sociology*, vol. xxii, no. 3, Sept. 1971, pp. 269–82.

ROBSON, R., 'Trinity College in the Age of Peel', *Ideas and Institutions of Victorian Britain*, ed. R. Robson, 1967, pp. 312–35.

STANLEY, A. P., 'Absolution', *Nineteenth Century*, vol. 3, Jan. 1878, pp. 183–95.

TOON, P., 'J. C. Ryle and Comprehensiveness', *Churchman*, vol. 89, no. 4, Oct.–Dec. 1975, pp. 280–3.

WALKER, R. B., 'Religious Changes in Liverpool in the 19th Century', *Journal of Ecclesiastical History*, vol. xix, no. 2, Oct. 1968, pp. 195–211.

WELCH, P., 'The Revival of an Active Convocation of Canterbury (1852–1855)', *Journal of Ecclesiastical History*, vol. 10, 1959, pp. 188–97.

WERLY, J., 'The Irish in Manchester, 1832–49', *Irish Historical Studies*, vol. xviii, no. 71, Mar. 1973, pp. 345–58.

WILSON, R., 'Ossington and the Denisons', *History Today*, Mar. 1968, pp. 164–72.

YOUSEFF, NADIA, 'Cultural Ideals, Feminine Behaviour and Family Control', *Comparative Studies in Science and History*, vol. 15, no. 3, June 1973, pp. 326–47.

PAMPHLETS

Anon., *A Letter on the Present State of Confusion in the Church of England*, by a Country Vicar, Rugeley, 1874.

—— *A Vindication from the Bible and the Book of Common Prayer of the Society of the Holy Cross*, by a Priest, 1877.

—— *Facts and Documents shewing the Alarming State of the Diocese of Oxford*, by a Senior Clergyman of the Diocese, 1859.

—— *Liberalism in the Priest's Craft*, by an elected Lay Representative, Manchester, n. d.

—— *Lord Selborne's Letter to the 'Times' and an Answer*, by a Layman (B.M.P.), 1874.

—— *Romanizing Germs: are there any in the Prayer-Book?* by a Clergyman, 1874.

—— *Quosque? How Far? How Long?* by a High Churchman of the Old School, 1873.

BARING, C. T., *A Charge delivered to the Clergy of the Diocese of Durham*, 1878.

BENNETT, W. J. E., *The Old Church Porch, IV*, 1862.

BLOMFIELD, C. J., *A Charge to the Clergy of London*, 1842.

BURGON, J. W., *Canon Robert Gregory, a Letter of Friendly Remonstrance*, 1881.

—— *Romanizing within the Church of England*, 1873.

CARTER, T. T., *The Freedom of Confession in the Church of England*, 1872.

—— *The Present Movement a True Phase of Anglo-Catholic Church Principles*, 1878.

CASTREE, G. H., *The Rev. Fr. Anderton, S.J., on the Miles Platting Case*, Manchester, 1883.

CLAUGHTON, T. L., *A Charge delivered to the Clergy and Churchwardens of the Diocese of St. Alban's*, 1878.

COX, J. B., *Correspondence between the Rt. Revd. the Lord Bishop of Liverpool and the Revd. J. Bell Cox*, Liverpool, 1880.

DALE, T. P., *The S. Vedast Case*, 1881.

DENISON, G. A., *A Charge of the Archdeacon of Taunton at his Visitation*, 1874.

—— *A Charge of the Archdeacon of Taunton at his Visitation, April 1877*, 1877.

—— *Why Should the Bishops continue to sit in the House of Lords?* 2nd edn., 1851.

DIGBY, G., *A Brief Address*, Harrogate, 1842.

DYKES, J. B., *Eucharistic Truth and Ritual*, 3rd edn., 1874.

EBURY, LORD, *Notes on the Declaration against a Revision of the Prayer-Book*, 2nd edn., 1860.

—— *On the Revision of the Liturgy*, 1860.

EGERTON, W., *Practical Readjustments of the Relation of the Church to the State*, 1877.

—— *Revision of the Rubrics*, 1874.

ENRAGHT, R. W., *A Pastoral to the Faithful Worshippers at Holy Trinity, Bordesley*, 1879.

—— *My Ordination Oaths . . . Am I Keeping Them?* 1880.

—— *Who are true Churchmen and Who are Conspirators?* n. d.

—— *My Prosecution under the Public Worship Regulation Act*, Birmingham, 1883.

FRASER, J., *A Charge delivered at his Primary Visitation*, Manchester, 1872.

—— *A Charge delivered at his Second Visitation*, 1876.

GLADSTONE, W. E., *The Church of England and Ritualism*, 1875.

GOODWIN, H., *Confession*, 1873.

GRINDLE, E. S., *Canon or Statute*, 1875.

HENSON, H. H., *Cui Bono: an Open Letter to Lord Halifax*, 1898.

HOLDEN, H. W., *The Coming Campaign: How it will be won*, 1874.

HUBBARD, J. G., *Ecclesiastical Courts, a letter to his Grace the Lord Archbishop of Canterbury*, 1880.

JACKSON, J., *Our Present Difficulties: a Charge delivered to the Clergy of the Diocese of London at his Second Visitation*, 1875.

LEE, F. G., *The Need of Spiritual Authority, a Sermon*, 1882.

LOWDER, C. F., *Sacramental Confession examined by Pastoral Experience*, 1874.

McCOLL, M., *The Advertisements of 1564, Fresh Evidence against the Purchas Judgement*, 1875.

MACKARNESS, J. F., *A Charge delivered to the Diocese of Oxford*, Oxford, 1872.

—— *A Plea for Toleration in answer to the No Popery Cry*, 1850.

MACKONOCHIE, A. H., *First Principles versus Erastianism*, 1876.

—— '*The Priest in Absolution*' *and the Society of the Holy Cross*, 1877.

MOBERLY, G., *A Charge to the Clergy*, 1873.

OAKLEY, J., *Correspondence between Prebendary Macdonald and the Dean of Manchester*, Manchester, 1885.

PELHAM, J. T., *A Charge delivered to the Clergy and Churchwardens in the Diocese of Norwich*, 1872.

PHILPOTT, H., *A Charge delivered to the Clergy and Churchwardens in the Diocese of Worcester*, 1877.

PRYNNE, G. R., *Private Confession, Penance, and Absolution authoritatively taught in the Church of England*, 1852.

PUSEY, E. B., *The Danger of Riches*, 1850.

—— *The Proposed Ecclesiastical Legislation*, 1874.

—— *Habitual Confession not discouraged by the Resolution accepted by the Lambeth Conference*, 1878.

RAMSEY, A. M., *Whose Hearts God has Touched*, 1961.

RIDSDALE, C. J., *The Ridsdale Judgement . . . to which is added a letter from the Revd. M. Woodward*, n. d.

ROGERS, J. G., *Antagonism and Litigation in the Established Church*, 1883.

RYLE, J. C., *A Charge, No. 1, delivered at his Primary Visitation*, 1881.

—— *A Charge, No. 2, delivered at his Primary Visitation*, 1881.

—— *Address on the Report of the Ecclesiastical Courts Commission*, 1883.

—— *Opening Address, Diocesan Conference*, 1883.

STEPHENS, A. J., *A Letter to His Grace the Lord Archbishop of York*, 1873.

—— and JEUNE, F., *The Public Worship Regulation Bill*, 1874.

STOWELL, T. A., *Lecture on Confession delivered in the Free Trade Hall, Manchester*, Manchester, 1858.

STREET, B., *In Search of Ritual*, 1867.

TOMLINSON, J. T., *The Literary Morality of the Ritualists*, 1867.

WAGNER, A. D., *Christ and Caesar Part II: a letter to the Lord Bishop of Chichester*, 1877.

—— *Reasons for Disobeying on Principle*, 2nd edn., 1874.

WILLIAMS, J. C., *The Demand for Freedom in the Church of England*, 1883.

WILSON, R. J., *An Earnest Protest*, Oxford, 1874.

WORDSWORTH, C., *A Plea for Toleration in Certain Ritual Matters*, 1874.

—— *States and Synods, their Respective Functions and Uses*, 1874.

BOOKS (place of publication is London unless otherwise stated).

ABERCROMBIE, N., *The Life and Work of Edmund Bishop*, 1959.

Annual Register 1874, 1875.

ANSON, P. F., *Fashions in Church Furnishings*, 1960.

—— *The Call of the Cloister*, 2nd edn., 1964.

Armstrong's Norfolk Diary, ed. H. B. J. Armstrong, 1963.

ARNSTEIN, W. L., *The Bradlaugh Case*, 1965.

ASHWELL, A. R., and WILBERFORCE, R. G., *Life of the Rt. Rev. Samuel Wilberforce*, revised edn., 3 vols., 1888.

ATLAY, J. B., *The Victorian Chancellors*, 2 vols., 1906–8.

AUSUBEL, H., *John Bright, Victorian Reformer*, New York, 1966.

AVERY, GILLIAN, *Victorian People*, 1970.

BAGEHOT, W., *Collected Works*, ed. N. St. John-Stevas, iii, 1968.

BALLEINE, G. R., *A History of the Evangelical Party*, 1908.

BARING-GOULD, S., *The Church Revival*, 1914.

BATTISCOMBE, G., *Shaftesbury, A Biography of the Seventh Earl, 1801–1885*, 1974.

BELL, G. K. A., *Randall Davidson Archbishop of Canterbury*, 2 vols., 1935.

BENSON, A. C., *Life and Letters of Maggie Benson*, 1917.

—— *The Life of E. W. Benson*, 2 vols., 1898.

BEST, G. F. A., *Shaftesbury*, 1964.

Letters of Lord Blachford, ed. G. E. Marindin, 1896.

BLAKE, R., *Disraeli*, 1966.

BLUNT, J. S., *Directorium Pastorale*, 1864.

BOYCE, E. J. A., *A Memorial of the Cambridge Camden Society*, 1888.

BOYCOTT, D. C. M., *The Secret History of the Oxford Movement*, 1933.

BRENDON, P., *Hawker of Morwenstow*, 1975.

BRIGHT, J., *Public Addresses*, ed. J. E. Thorold Rogers, 1879.

—— *The Diaries of John Bright*, ed. R. A. J. Walling, 1930.

BROWN, C. K. F., *A History of the English Clergy*, 1953.

BROWN, H. MILES, *The Church in Cornwall*, Truro, 1964.

BRYCE, J., *Studies in Contemporary Biography*, 1903.

BURGON, J. W., *Lives of Twelve Good Men*, 2 vols., 1888.

BURNARD, F., *Records and Reminiscences*, 1917.

CALDER-MARSHALL, A., *The Enthusiast*, 1962.

CARPENTER, W. B., *History of the Church of England*, 1919.

The Diary of Lady Frederick Cavendish, ed. J. Bailey, 1927.

CECIL, LADY G., *Life of Robert Marquis of Salisbury*, 4 vols., 1921–32.

CHADWICK, O., *Edward King, Bishop of Lincoln, 1885–1910*, Lincoln, 1968.

—— *The Founding of Cuddesdon*, 1954.

—— *The Mind of the Oxford Movement*, 1960.

CHADWICK, O., *The Victorian Church*, 3rd edn., 1971.

CHURCH, MARY C., *Life and Letters of Dean Church*, 1895.

CHURCH, R. W., *Occasional Papers*, 2 vols., 1897.

CHURCHILL, R. S., *Winston S. Churchill*, i, 1966.

CLARKE, C. S., and WEEKS, G. E. A. (eds.), *The Protestant Dictionary*, 1933.

CLARKE, G. KITSON, *The Making of Victorian England*, 1962.

COCKSHUT, A. O. J., *Anglican Attitudes: A Study of Victorian Religious Controversies*, 1959.

—— *Truth to Life: The Art of Biography in the Nineteenth Century*, 1974.

COLLINGWOOD, S. D., *The Life and Letters of Lewis Carroll*, 1898.

COWLING, M., *1867: Disraeli, Gladstone and Revolution*, 1967.

CREIGHTON, L., *Life and Letters of Mandell Creighton*, 2 vols., 1904.

—— and LIVINGSTONE, E. A. (eds.), *The Oxford Dictionary of the Christian Church*, 2nd edn., 1974.

DALE, H. P., *The Life and Letters of T. P. Dale*, 2 vols., 1894.

DAVIDSON, R. T., and BENHAM, W., *Life of Archibald Campbell Tait, Archbishop of Canterbury*, 2 vols., 1891.

DENISON, G. A., *Notes of My Life, 1805–1878*, 2nd edn., 1878.

DENISON, H. P., *Seventy-two Years Church Recollections*, 1925.

DENISON, L. E., *Fifty Years at East Brent*, 1902.

DERRY, J. W., *The Radical Tradition*, 1967.

DIGGLE, J. W., *The Lancashire Life of Bishop Fraser*, 1889.

DISRAELI, B., *Letters to Lady Bradford and Lady Chesterfield*, ed. the Marquess of Zetland, 2 vols., 1929.

—— *Tancred: or, The New Crusade*, 1847.

DUGDALE, B. E. C., *Arthur James Balfour*, 2 vols., 1936.

DURANDUS, W., *The Symbolism of Churches and Church Ornaments*, trans. J. M. Neale and B. Webb, 1843.

EDE, J. F., *History of Wednesbury*, Birmingham, 1962.

EDWARDS, D. L., *Leaders of the Church of England, 1828–1944*, 1971.

ELLIOTT-BINNS, L. E., *Religion in the Victorian Era*, 2nd edn., 1964.

ELVEY, J. M., *Recollections of the Cathedral and Parish Church of Manchester*, Manchester, 1913.

EMBRY, J., *The Catholic Movement and the S.S.C.*, 1931.

ENRAGHT, R. W., *Catholic Worship*, 1871.

ESCOTT, T. H. S., *Platform, Press, Politics, and Play*, Bristol, n. d.

EVANS, S. G., *The Social Hope of the Christian Church*, 1965.

FRERE, W. H., *Walter Howard Frere: His Correspondence on Liturgical Revision and Construction*, ed. R. C. D. Jasper, 1954.

FROUDE, J. A., *Short Studies on Great Subjects*, new edn., 4 vols., 1893.

GARDINER, A. G., *Life of Sir William Harcourt*, 2 vols., 1923.

GASH, N., *Sir Robert Peel: The Life of Sir Robert Peel after 1830*, 1972.

GATHORNE-HARDY, A. E., *Gathorne-Hardy, First Earl of Cranbrook*, 2 vols., 1910.

GILBERT, E. W., *Brighton*, 1954.

GLADSTONE, C., *Mary Drew*, 1919.

GLADSTONE, W. E., *The Gladstone Diaries:* Vol. I, *1825–1832*, ed. M. R. D. Foot, 1968.

—— *The Gladstone Diaries:* Vol. III, *1840–1847*, ed. M. R. D. Foot and H. C. G. Matthew, 1974.

—— *Letters on Church and Religion*, ed. D. C. Lathbury, 2 vols., 1910.

GOOCH, G. P., *History and Historians in the Nineteenth Century*, 2nd edn., 1952.

HAYES, L. M., *Reminiscences of Manchester from the Year 1840*, Manchester, 1905.

Letters of Herbert Hensley Henson, ed. E. F. Braley, 1951.

HERMELINCK, H., *Das Christentum in der Menschheitsgeschichte von der Französischen Revolution bis zur Gegenwart*, Tübingen, iii, 1953.

HEYWOOD, T. P., *Reminiscences, Letters and Journals of T. P. Heywood, Bart.*, ed. his daughter, Manchester, 1899.

Hierurgia Anglicana, the Cambridge Camden Society, 1845, etc.

HODDER, E., *The Life and Work of the Seventh Earl of Shaftesbury*, Popular edn., 1893.

HOLLAND, H. S., *Personal Studies*, n. d.

Henry Scott Holland, Memoir and Letters, ed. S. Paget, 1921.

The Letters of A. E. Housman, ed. H. Maas, 1971.

HUDSON, D., *Munby, Man of Two Worlds*, 1972.

HUGHES, T., *James Fraser, Second Bishop of Manchester*, 1887.

HUTCHINGS, W. H., *Life and Letters of T. T. Carter*, 1903.

INGLIS, K. S., *The Churches and the Working Classes in Victorian England*, 1963.

JOHNSTON, J. O., *Life and Letters of Henry Parry Liddon*, 1904.

KEBLE, J., *The Christian Year*, 1827.

KEMP, E. W., *Counsel and Consent*, 1961.

KEMPSON, F. C., *The Church in Modern England*, 1908.

KINGSLEY, C., *Yeast: a Problem*, 1851.

KITCHIN, G. W., *Edward Harold Browne, D.D.*, 1895.

KNOX, E. A., *Reminiscences of an Octogenarian, 1847–1934*, 1934.

LIDDON, H. P., *Life of E. B. Pusey, D.D.*, 4 vols., 1893–7.

LOANE, M. L., *John Charles Ryle, 1816–1900*, 1953.

LOCKHART, J. G., *Charles Lindley Viscount Halifax*, 2 vols., 1935–6.

LONGFORD, E., *Victoria R.I.*, 1964.

LOUISE, M., *My Memories of Six Reigns*, 1956.

LOUTH, A. G., *The Influence of J. M. Neale*, 1962.

LOUTH, A. G., *John Mason Neale: Priest Extraordinary*, 1975.

LOW, S., and SANDERS, L. C., *The Political History of England*, vol. xii, 1913.

LOWDER, C. F., *Twenty-One Years in St. George's Mission*, 1877.

LUCY, H. W., *A Diary of Two Parliaments, the Disraeli Parliament, 1874–1880*, 2nd edn., 1885.

MACDONNELL, J. C., *Life and Correspondence of William Connor Magee*, 2 vols., 1896.

McCARTHY, J., *A History of Our Own Times*, 4 vols., 1879–80.

McGONAGALL, W., *Poetic Gems*, 1934.

MACKENZIE, C., *On Moral Courage*, 1962.

Alexander Heriot Mackonochie, a Memoir by E.A.T., ed. E. F. Russell, 1890.

MAGNUS, P., *Gladstone: A Biography*, 1954.

MARSH, P. T., *The Victorian Church in Decline*, 1969.

MEACHAM, STANDISH, *Lord Bishop, the Life of Samuel Wilberforce, 1805–1873*, Cambridge, Mass., 1970.

MILLS, A. R., *Two Victorian Ladies*, 1969.

MONYPENNY, W. F., and BUCKLE, G. E., *Life of Disraeli*, new edn., 2 vols., 1929.

MORISON, S., *History of The Times*, vol. ii, 1939.

MORLEY, J., *Life of Gladstone*, 3 vols., 1903.

MOULE, H. C. G., *The Supper of the Lord*, 1882.

NEALE, J. M., *Sequentiae ex missalibus . . . Recensuit, notulisque instruxit J. M. Neale*, 1852.

—— *Carols for Christmastide, set to ancient melodies*, 1853.

—— *Mediaeval Hymns and Sequences*, trans. J. M. Neale, 1867.

—— *Sermons on the Song of Songs*, 1867.

—— and LITTLEDALE, R. F., *The Private Devotions of Lancelot Andrewes*, new edn., 1898.

NEWMAN, J. H., *Apologia Pro Vita Sua*, 1864.

—— *Difficulties of Anglicans*, 1850.

—— *Lectures on the Prophetical Office of the Church*, 1837.

—— *Parochial and Plain Sermons*, vol. i, 1908 edn.

—— *Newman: Prose and Poetry*, ed. G. Tillotson, 1957.

OLLARD, S. L., CROSSE, G., and BOND, M. F., *A Dictionary of English Church History*, 2nd edn., 1919.

OLLARD, S. L., *The Anglo-Catholic Revival*, 1925.

—— *The Oxford Movement*, 1915.

OVERTON, J. H., and WORDSWORTH, ELIZABETH, *Christopher Wordsworth Bishop of Lincoln*, 1888.

PALMER, R., *Memorials Part II: Personal and Political, 1865–1895*, vol. i, 1898.

PARISH, W. D., *A Dictionary of the Sussex Dialect*, Lewes, 1875.

PAUL, H. W., *A History of Modern England*, 5 vols., 1904–6.

PERRY-GORE, G., *The Oldham Chapelry*, Oldham, 1906.

PEVSNER, N., *North Somerset and Bristol*, 1958.

PHILLIMORE, R., *The Ecclesiastical Law of the Church of England*, 2nd edn., 2 vols., 1895.

PONSONBY, A., *Henry Ponsonby*, 1942.

PROTHERO, R., and BRADLEY, G. G., *Life and Correspondence of A. P. Stanley*, 3rd edn., 2 vols., 1894.

PRYNNE, G. R., *The Eucharistic Manual*, 2nd edn., 1866.

PURCELL, E. S., *The Life of H. E. Cardinal Manning*, 2 vols., 1896.

QUECKETT, W., *My Sayings and Doings*, 1888.

RECKITT, M. B. (ed.), *For Christ and the People*, 1968.

REYNOLDS, M., *Martyr of Ritualism*, 1965.

RIDLEY, J., *Lord Palmerston*, Panther edn., 1972.

ROSCOE, E. S. (ed.), *The Bishop of Lincoln's Case*, 1891.

RUSSELL, G. W. E., *Arthur Stanton, a Memoir*, 1917.

—— *Dr. Liddon*, 1905.

—— *Edward King, Sixtieth Bishop of Lincoln*, 1912.

—— *Malcolm McColl, Memoirs and Correspondence*, 1914.

—— *St. Alban the Martyr: a History of Fifty Years*, 1913.

RYAN, M., *The Philosophy of Marriage*, 1839.

RYLE, J. C., *Principles for Churchmen*, 4th edn., 1900.

Lord Salisbury on Politics, ed. P. Smith, 1972.

SCHAEFER, P., *The Catholic Regeneration of the Church of England*, English trans. 1935.

SHANNON, R. T., *Gladstone and the Bulgarian Agitation of 1876*, 1963.

SHAW, W. A., *Manchester Old and New*, 2 vols., 1894.

SMITH, B. A., *Dean Church*, 1958.

SMITH, H. KIRK, *William Thomson, Archbishop of York*, 1958.

SPURGEON, C. H., *The Treasury of the New Testament*, n. d.

STÄHLIN, W., *Via Vitae, Lebenserrinerungen*, Kassel, 1968.

STANLEY, A. P., *The Life and Correspondence of Thomas Arnold, D.D.*, 2nd edn., 1890.

STONE, D. (ed.), *The Deposited Prayer Book, by a Group of Priests*, 1927.

STRATFORD, E. W., *The Victorian Sunset*, 1931.

STREET, H., *Freedom, the Individual and the Law*, 3rd edn., 1972.

Letters of William Stubbs, Bishop of Oxford, 1825–1901, ed. W. H. Hutton, 1904.

TAYLOR, A. J. P., *The Trouble Makers*, 1957.

Memoirs of Archbishop Temple, ed. E. G. Sandford, 2 vols., 1906.

THACKERAY, W. M., *Roundabout Papers, Works*, xii, 1898.

TRAILL, H. D., and MANN, J. S. (eds.), *Social England*, xi, 1904.

TUCKER, H. W., *The Life and Episcopate of G. A. Selwyn*, 2 vols., 1879.

VEBLEN, T., *The Theory of the Leisure Class*, Unwin edn., 1970.

VICTORIA, QUEEN, *Dearest Child, Letters between Queen Victoria and the Princess Royal*, ed. R. Fulford, 1964.

—— *Letters of Queen Victoria*, 2nd ser., ed. G. E. Buckle, 1926, etc.

VINCENT, J. R., *How the Victorians Voted*, 1967.

—— *The Formation of the British Liberal Party, 1857–68*, Pelican edn., 1972.

VOLL, D., *Catholic Evangelicalism: The Acceptance of Evangelical Traditions by the Oxford Movement during the Second Half of the Nineteenth Century*, trans. V. Ruffer, 1963.

WALKER, C., *The Ritual Reason Why*, 1866.

WARD, W., *Life of John Henry Cardinal Newman*, 1912.

WATSON, E. W., *Life of Bishop John Wordsworth*, 1915.

WHITE, J. E., *The Cambridge Movement*, 1962.

WILDE, J. P., BARON PENZANCE, *The Bacon–Shakespeare Controversy: a judicial summing-up*, ed. M. H. Kinnear, 1902.

WRIGHT, C. H. H., and NEIL, C., *A Protestant Dictionary*, 1904.

YOUNG, G. M., *Victorian England, Portrait of an Age*, 2nd edn., 1953.

INDEX

St. Mary, Tedburn, 120
St. Mary Magdalene's, Paddington, 26
St. Paul's Cathedral, 71, 87
St. Peter's, London Docks, 18, 26, 113
St. Peter's, Folkestone, 97
St. Peter's, Swinton, 27
St. Peter-at-Gowts, Lincoln, 117, 119
St. Thomas Aquinas, 11
St. Vedast's, Foster Lane, 102
St. Vincent de Paul, 28
Salford, 10, 30, 106
Salisbury, Lady G., 125
Salisbury, 3rd Marquess of, viii–ix, 11,
    15, 40, 48, 52, 55f., 58, 60 n. 1, 68,
    71–3, 74 and n. 4, 77, 114, 123, 127
Samuelson, H. B., 88
Sanday, Revd. W., 128 and n. 2
Sandon, Lord, 11, 53, 76, 115
Sankey, I. D., 10
Sargant, Revd. H. M., 26
Scotland, 25, 76f.
Scott, Lord H., 67
Scottish Patronage Bill, 67
Selborne, Earl of, 81f., 98, 100 n. 1, 111
Selwyn, G. A., Bishop of Lichfield, 80f.,
    99, 103, 108
Sexuality, Victorian, 33f.
Shannon, R. T., 58 n. 1
Shaftesbury, 7th Earl of, 8f., 34, 37,
    40–2, 55–60, 67, 69 and n. 3, 72, 74
Sheffield, 86
Shipley, Revd. O., 31
Sisterhoods, 14f., 24, 26, 28, 73, 102
Six Points, 21–3, fig. 1
Sligo, Marquess of, 4
Slope, Revd. O., 2, 14
Slums, 9, 17, 91
Smith, Revd. S., 53
Social Class, 23f., 24 n. 1, 86f., 89–93,
    106, 127f. See also Middle Classes,
    Upper Classes, Working Classes
Social problems, 90–3, 105f.
Socialism, 90–3, 95
Society of the Holy Cross, 27f., 31, 93
Southey, R., 14
Spurgeon, Revd. C. H., 10
Stählin, W., Bishop of Oldenburg, 95f.
Stained glass, 4
Stanhope, 5th Earl, 59
Stanley, Very Revd. A. P., Dean of
    Westminster, 1f., 49, 117, 125
Stanton, Revd. A. H., 52, 93f.
Star Chamber, 127
State, and church, 16–8, 41, 44, 61, 65,
    78, 93–6, 127
Stations of the Cross, 28
Stead, W. T., 89 n. 2
Stephen, J. F., 97
Stephens, A. J., 97
Stowell, Revd. H., 10, 31f.

Stuart, House of, 75
Stubbs, W., Bishop of Oxford, 4, 114,
    118, 127f.
Suffragan sees, 5
Sumner, J. B., Archbishop of Canter-
    bury, 16
Sunday Schools, 6, 47
Superstition, 1, 7, 13
Surplice, 16f., 26, 43, 98
Suspension, of clergymen, 5, 30, 42,
    100, 137
Sussex, 28
Symbolism, 3, 27, 42, 61, 124
The Symbolism of Churches and Church
    Ornaments, by W. Durandus, 14, 27

Tabernacle, 111
Tait, A. C., Archbishop of Canterbury,
    vii–ix, 8, 18, 30, 35, 37, 39, 41f.,
    44–61, 69–73, 80f., 83–5, 87, 94, 97,
    99f., 102–4, 110f., 113f., 116, 121,
    123, 125, 127, figs. 5, 6 and 7
Talbot, J. G., 67, 72, 77, 113
Tancred: or, The New Crusade, by
    B. Disraeli, 7
Taunton, 53
Taylor, A. J. P., 87 n. 3
Taylor, P. A., 78
Teignmouth, Lord, 75
Temple, F., Archbishop of Canterbury,
    40, 45, 113, 118
Thackeray, W. M., 1
Theological Colleges, 20f., 117
Thirlwall, C., Bishop of St. David's, 36
Thirty-nine Articles, 8, 12, 36, 84,
    fig. 4
Thomson, W., Archbishop of York, 23,
    31, 42, 49, 56f., 59, 61, 63, 69–71, 81,
    83, 105, 110, 113f.
Thorold, A. W., Bishop of Rochester,
    118
Thorp, Revd. T., 27
The Times, viii, 47, 50, 52, 72, 81, 102,
    112, 120
Thynne, Lord H., 77
Toleration, 12, 35, 43f., 44 n. 5, 63, 127
Tooth, Revd. A., 25, 27, 100–2
Toryism, 7, 52, 77, 91, 115, 123
Townroe, Revd. J. W. (Townsend in
    text), 119
Tract 90, by J. H. Newman, 8
Tractarians, 1–3, 11, 20, 23, 25–8, 50,
    75, 82, 89 n. 5, 103, 123, 128
Trades unions, 92f.
Trinity College, Cambridge, 27 and
    n. 2, 77f.
Tritton, H., 4
Trollope, A., 2, 14
Truro, diocese of, 5
Turks, 79, 87

INDEX